CREDIT UNION
TELLER HANDBOOK

THIRD EDITION

Produced by the Center for Professional Development,
CUNA & Affiliates
Madison, Wisconsin

Product #22823

Catherine M. Izor

CUNA & Affiliates

KENDALL/HUNT PUBLISHING COMPANY
4050 Westmark Drive   Dubuque, Iowa 52002

With respect to the content of this manuscript, neither Credit Union National Association, Inc. (CUNA) nor any of its affiliates or its or their respective employees make any express or implied warranty or assume any legal liability or responsibility for the accuracy, completeness, or usefulness of any information, commercial product, service, process, provider, vendor, or trade name/mark that is disclosed. References to any specific commercial product, service, process, provider, vendor, or trade name/mark in this manuscript also does not necessarily constitute or imply that such product or provider is endorsed, recommended, or warranted by CUNA. The views and opinions of the authors expressed herein do not necessarily state or reflect those of CUNA and such reference shall not be used for advertising or product endorsement purposes.

This publication is designed to provide accurate and authoritative information in regard to the subject matter covered. It is sold with the understanding that the publisher, Credit Union National Association, Inc., is not engaged in rendering legal, accounting, or other professional services. If legal advice or other expert assistance is required, the services of a competent professional should be sought.

—From a Declaration of Principles jointly adopted by a Committee of the American Bar Association and a Committee of Publishers and Associations.

Written by Catherine M. Izor
Editor/Third Edition: Karen Bankston
Contributor/Third Edition: Ruth Witzeling
Produced by Jeremiah Cahill

Copyright © 2000
Credit Union National Association, Inc.

ISBN 0-7872-6622-1

All rights reserved. No part of this publication may be reproduced, stored in a retrieval system, or transmitted, in any form or by any means, electronic, mechanical, photocopying, recording, or otherwise, without the prior written permission of the copyright owner.

Printed in the United States of America
10   9   8   7   6   5   4   3   2   1

CONTENTS

ACKNOWLEDGMENTS

The author expresses special thanks to the following people for their suggestions and review of this handbook: Shirley Baker, Texas D.P.S. Credit Union; Kimberly M. Davis, Dupont Fibers Federal Credit Union; Veneta Johnston, Tech Federal Credit Union; Jean Simon, Tucson Healthcare Federal Credit Union; and Alice Swartzfager, Clarion University Federal Credit Union.

INTRODUCTION

Financial services have changed a great deal in the last twenty years. Consumers have more choices than ever before, and an increasing number handle their financial accounts via ATMs, phone centers, and Internet "branches." The vast majority of credit union members, however, continue to conduct their financial business in person at their local branch. As a credit union teller or member service representative, you are the most familiar face to those members. You are a helper and problem solver. Members count on you for accuracy, courtesy, and professionalism. For many members, you are the credit union.

This handbook will help you prepare for those roles. It includes the basic information you need to get started and to succeed in your position. It is excellent preparation for the more advanced training your credit union or league will provide.

In this handbook you'll find a brief overview of general concepts and skills, an explanation of your most important duties and responsibilities, and useful techniques for achieving success in your job. At the end of each chapter you'll also find several activities and checklists to help you apply your learning to your job. These activities will reinforce key concepts, help you identify your strengths and skills to improve, and provide a method for communicating with your supervisor. They will also make it easy for you to tailor the information you learn here to specific conditions in your credit union.

- Chapter 1 introduces the credit union movement and the teller's role in relation to members and fields of membership.
- Chapter 2 reviews the basic products and services that credit unions typically offer members. You'll also read about your responsibilities in regard to these services.
- Chapter 3 lists tips for good communication with members.
- Chapter 4 reviews techniques for establishing and maintaining good relationships with coworkers and supervisors.
- Chapter 5 explains effective methods for handling cash, share drafts, and checks.

- Chapter 6 emphasizes security measures—the internal controls of your credit union and how you can help prevent fraud in transactions.
- Chapter 7 presents suggestions on how to handle several credit union emergencies, including robberies, natural disasters, fires, and bomb threats.
- Chapter 8 provides ideas for developing the qualities and skills that will give you future success.

The usefulness of this handbook depends on you. Read it, interpret it, make it a part of your daily work, and keep it for handy reference. Mark sections you need to learn more about. Write questions in the margins. Underline points you consider most valuable. Learn the policies and procedures required in your credit union. And take advantage of additional training opportunities. Then, put the information to use on the job.

In addition, many other resources are available that tell the credit union story and provide further training. Your supervisor can help you with print, video, and other training formats when you're ready to advance.

Best wishes for your personal growth and professional development as a credit union employee!

YOUR ROLE AS A CREDIT UNION TELLER

"Just turn right at the corner. You can drop me by the mailbox. I'm even a little early. Thanks for dropping me off for my first day of work, Mom."

"I'll pick you up, too. I want to hear all about it. We're big credit union supporters in our family, you know. Grandpa was one of the first directors when his plant started a credit union."

"Yeah, he said so at the family reunion when I told him I got this job as a teller. But you know, I'm still not sure I understand the big deal about credit unions. What's the difference between this place and a bank?"

"I'm sure you'll find that out in the coming weeks, honey. But Grandpa would be happy to tell you about it from his point of view, too."

"Yeah, I bet he would. Hey, maybe I'll be his teller the next time he stops here!"

"That would make his day. Good luck, honey!"

Some of the first questions you (or people you know) may have had when you started this job are:

- What is a credit union?
- Is it different from a bank?
- Is being a teller at a credit union different from being a teller at a bank?

Many people who begin working as a credit union teller have these questions, so that's where this book begins. In this chapter, you'll get an overview of the credit union movement and what it means to be a teller here. In the rest of the book, you'll explore more specific parts of your job, such as services, member relations, employee relations, cash and check handling, security, and other responsibilities.

What Is a Credit Union?

Credit unions are a special type of financial institution. They are *cooperatives*, and that makes them unique. Three aspects define a credit union:

- member ownership and control
- not-for-profit orientation
- volunteer involvement

In addition to these fundamental principles, credit unions also comply with various types of government regulations. Let's look at each of these areas in more detail.

Member Ownership and Control

When people say, "This is *my* credit union," they mean it. Unlike other financial institutions, a credit union is owned and operated by the people it serves. All credit unions were originally formed by a group of people who decided they wanted to control their own financial destiny. These people—members, not customers—provided the initial capital to start the credit union, pool their money as savings, and make low-cost loans to each other. This is where the idea of credit unions as "people helping people" comes from.

But how does this initial group get together? What makes members a group? People who formed a particular credit union had something in common, such as working for the same employer or living in the same community. Some credit unions have been formed by people who worship together. In addition, many credit unions have expanded to include several defined groups of people in their **field of membership.** This makes it possible for several groups, such as employee groups from different small companies, to band together and gain access to credit union membership. Otherwise, it might be difficult or even impossible for each employee group to operate a credit union on its own.

Every credit union in the world—including yours—started this way, and the principle of self-help still applies, no matter how large or how small your credit union is now. All credit unions are organized as **cooperatives.** That means they are owned and controlled by the people who use the services—the members. That's why the individuals who come to your teller window are called **members,** not customers. They are actually both customers and owners through their credit union membership.

Each member has one vote—no matter how much or how little money that member deposits or borrows.

When people become members, they assume responsibilities for the democratic control of the credit union. These responsibilities are apparent when members use mail ballots to elect directors. And they are apparent at your annual meeting where members meet to hear reports of board and committee members and vote on credit union issues. Each member has one vote—no matter how much or how little money is deposited or borrowed.

Your members also play a key role in setting policy. They elect directors who appoint other members to committees and hire managers to handle day-to-day operations. Figure 1.1 shows a typical credit union organizational chart.

Member-ownership is a key difference between credit unions and other types of financial institutions. These other organizations are owned by investors or stockholders who may or may not use the services of the financial institution.

Not-for-Profit Orientation

Another key characteristic of a credit union is a not-for-profit orientation. No, this doesn't mean that a credit union loses money. This simply means that after normal operating expenses are paid and funds are set aside for reserves, any net income that remains is returned to the members as attractive dividends on their savings, reduced interest rates on loans, and/or improved services. In contrast, other organizations that are owned by investors generally distribute part of the profits to the stockholders as a return on their investment. (See figure 1.2 for a comparison for various ways credit unions and other financial services providers differ.)

Figure 1.1 Typical Credit Union Organizational Structure

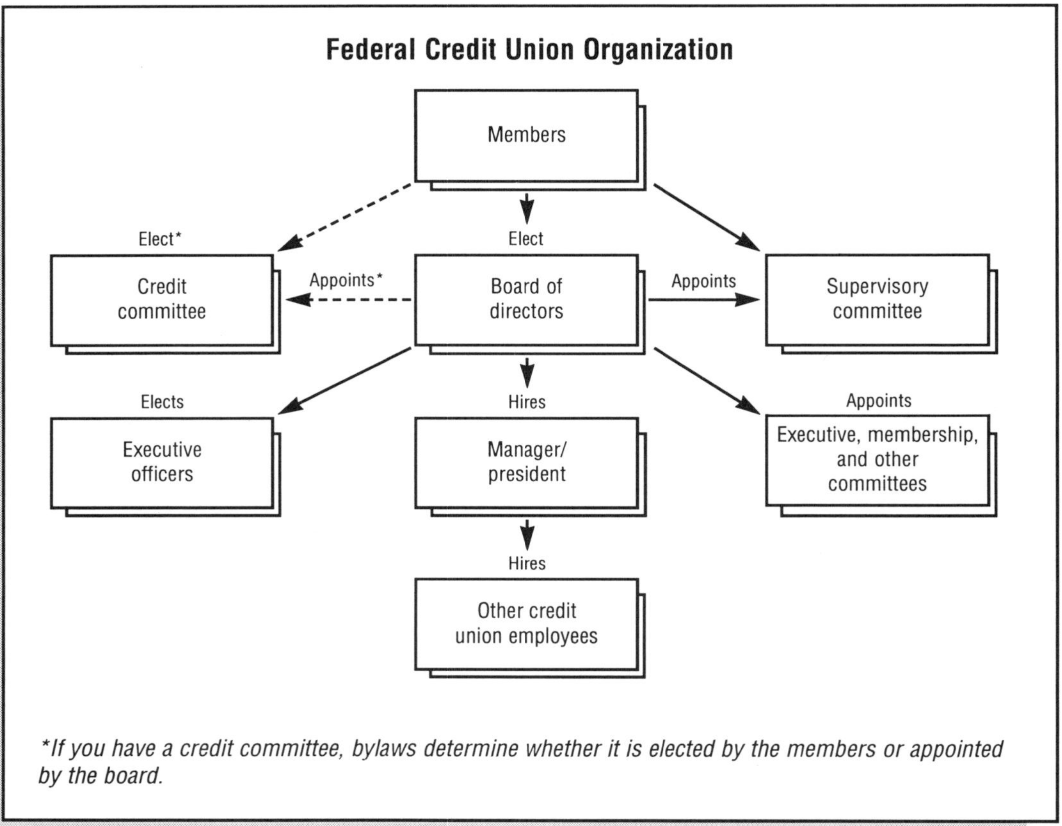

Federal Credit Union Organization

Members

Elect* — Elect — (to Supervisory committee)

Credit committee ← Appoints* — Board of directors — Appoints → Supervisory committee

Elects — Hires — Appoints

Executive officers ← Manager/ president → Executive, membership, and other committees

↓ Hires

Other credit union employees

If you have a credit committee, bylaws determine whether it is elected by the members or appointed by the board.

Volunteer Involvement

Your board of directors and committee members volunteer their time to fulfill the expectations of your membership, ensure quality service, and maintain financial safety and soundness. These volunteers are unique in the financial world in that they assume tremendous responsibilities and demanding workloads—in most cases without monetary compensation. They contribute their time, expertise, and energy to the ideal of mutual self-help through credit unions.

Figure 1.2 How Credit Unions Compare

The Credit Union as a Financial Institution

	Credit Unions	Banks	Savings & Loan Associations	Small Loan Companies	Retail Store Charge Accounts
Orientation	Service	Profit	Profit	Profit	Profit
Owners	Members, who use the services	Shareholders, who may not be customers	Shareholders, who may not be customers	Shareholders, who may not be customers	Shareholders, who may not be customers
Type of Organization	State or federally chartered cooperative	State or federally chartered corporation	State or federally chartered corporation	Corporation	Local or national corporation
Source of Income	Loans to members, investments, fees	Loans to customers, investments, fees	Loans to customers, investments, fees	Loans to customers, fees	Loans to customers, fees
Distribution of Income	Dividends to members	Dividends to stockholders	Dividends to stockholders	Dividends to corporation's investors	Dividends to store's stockholders
Services Offered	Primarily consumer savings and lending plans, transaction services, etc.	Business and consumer savings and lending plans, transaction services, etc.	Business and consumer savings and lending plans, transaction services, etc.	Consumer lending plans	Consumer lending plans to purchase items in the store

Government Regulation

Beyond volunteer commitment and dedicated credit union management, members have an additional source of protection for their funds and the continued safe operation of the credit union. Credit unions are *regulated* by government agencies. This means that the government agencies are responsible for supervising credit unions and making sure they follow certain rules and operate safely.

How does this work? Before a credit union can open for business, it must obtain a **charter,** or license to operate, from the government. A credit union must meet certain requirements and standards before it will be granted a charter. Credit unions can be chartered by either the state or federal government. If yours is a state-chartered credit union, it is supervised primarily by your state regulatory agency. The agency examines your credit union regularly to make sure it is complying with all appropriate laws and regulations and is being operated in a sound and prudent manner. If yours is a federal credit union (all federal credit unions have the word *federal* in their names), it is regulated and examined periodically by the federal agency called the National Credit Union Administration (NCUA).

All federally chartered credit unions are required to provide insurance on deposits up to $100,000. All federal and many state-chartered credit unions are insured by the National Credit Union Share Insurance Fund (NCUSIF). Other state-chartered credit unions are insured by various state and regional cooperative share insurers; most of these insurers provide the same levels of coverage as the NCUSIF.

YOU'RE PART OF A LARGER CREDIT UNION MOVEMENT

Your credit union may be only one of many financial institutions in the city or area where you're located. But each credit union is also part of a larger national and international network. This network is made up of membership and service organizations at all levels (see figure 1.3). Through the credit union system, your members are connected with people all over the globe who are trying to make their lives better.

(See appendix A for information on the affiliated credit union organizations listed in figure 1.3.)

THE ROLES OF A CREDIT UNION TELLER

Now that you have an overview of how your credit union is different from other financial institutions, let's look at your role as a teller in your credit union.

Your Role Regarding Members

Credit unions exist to serve their members' financial needs. As a teller, you are in the best position to fulfill that mission. While each staff person plays a vital part

Figure 1.3 Credit Union System

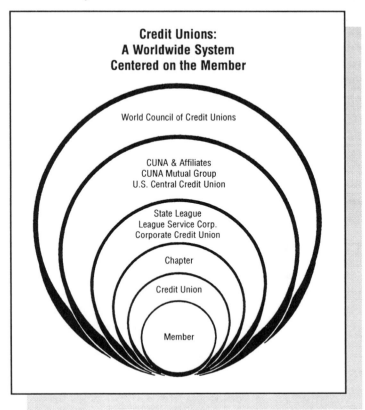

**Credit Unions:
A Worldwide System
Centered on the Member**

World Council of Credit Unions

CUNA & Affiliates
CUNA Mutual Group
U.S. Central Credit Union

State League
League Service Corp.
Corporate Credit Union

Chapter

Credit Union

Member

in the credit union's success, you hold the anchor position on the credit union's team of employees.

> *To many members*, you *are the credit union.*

You are in direct contact with members every hour the credit union is open. You are the employee members are likely to deal with most often. Consequently, you play a major role in the credit union's relationship with its members. In fact, to many members, *you* are the credit union.

Your role to members is that of ambassador, teacher, and service provider. As ambassador, you represent the credit union—its democratic, cooperative spirit, its friendly, personal nature, and its people-first philosophy. As teacher, you explain policies that are established not to hinder but to help members by protecting their accounts. You also educate members on the credit union's philosophy and help them learn the fundamental differences that set credit unions apart from other financial institutions. In addition, you introduce them to a variety of financial services that can benefit them.

As service provider, you not only carry out members' requests, you point out additional services that may help them as well. You handle members' financial accounts with accuracy and professionalism and protect their funds by helping to prevent fraud. Another key part of your position is to obtain answers from the credit union's "back-office" technical experts when members have a question or problem. Overall, your job is much more than just handling deposits and withdrawals. Figure 1.4 outlines typical teller duties.

Your Role in Other Departments

As a teller you wear many hats when working with members, but your job does not end there. You also have responsibilities to every other department, or functional area, in the credit union. All credit union employees must cooperate if the organization is to succeed. You and each of your fellow employees share a common goal—to serve members.

Practice Teamwork

A team works best when players know the ground rules and understand the jobs each teammate performs. The same applies to you as a teller. Each transaction you conduct is governed by your credit union's policies and procedures. With each transaction, you interact with one or more other credit union departments. It's essential, then, that you understand your credit union's policies and procedures and what functions other departments handle.

A team works best when players know the ground rules and understand the job each teammate performs.

Knowing how other departments function will make you more valuable as an employee. Instead of simply memorizing procedures, you need to understand the impact those procedures have throughout the credit union and the reasons they

Figure 1.4 Daily Responsibilities of a Credit Union Teller

Being a teller involves a blend of technical and people skills. Here are some of your key responsibilities:

- Handle transactions accurately and efficiently.
- Inform members about products and services that may save them time and/or money or increase their earnings.
- Answer members' questions about account balances and other information.
- Find answers for members about how services work (and/or why they're not working the way members expect).
- Follow up with members if answers are not immediately available.
- Help create a friendly, courteous atmosphere.
- Evaluate transactions for potential fraud.
- Track down the cause of errors and correct them.
- Maintain confidentiality.
- Ensure compliance with policies, procedures, and laws.
- Balance your work, and help balance the branch or credit union.
- Fulfill other shared responsibilities, such as ordering supplies, updating rate boards, refilling brochure racks, filing signature cards, etc.

should be followed. In addition, the information will help you answer members' questions about their accounts.

Members often expect tellers to handle all their needs at the counter. Whenever possible, this should be done. But no employee knows everything. Even with a solid understanding of each department, you will occasionally hear a question you can't answer. When that happens, it's much better to get help than to give incorrect information.

Know the Other Departments

As a teller, you are part of the credit union's member service function. This function, or department, may also include specialized representatives who help members open new accounts and employees who work in call centers, serving members who prefer to conduct their financial business by phone. Depending on their size, most credit unions also have these departments: accounting, share draft, payroll deduction, loans, investments, collections, human resources, information services, and marketing. Instead of separate departments, smaller credit unions may have individual employees who handle these functions. A brief explanation of each function follows.

Every transaction you complete must be double-checked and reported by the **accounting department.** With the help of the credit union's data processing system, accounting employees make sure all transactions are classified into categories and posted in the credit union's general ledger. You must help this department by striving for accuracy in all transactions and identifying and helping to correct problems with member accounts.

The **share draft department** tracks members' share draft accounts by performing such duties as ordering new share drafts, placing stop payments, handling overdrafts, and working with monthly statements. At the teller window, you may hear questions about share draft accounts that require assistance. Your first response is to try to help. If the problem requires research or you are unsure of how to solve it, be aware of who can help and call that person immediately. Or, direct the member to the appropriate location.

In addition, find out which share draft transactions you may be able to complete at the counter to save members time. For example, at your credit union, tellers may have authority to take stop-payment requests and forward them directly to the share draft department. This saves members from having to wait until a share draft employee can help them.

The **payroll deduction department,** which may be part of the accounting department, is responsible for tracking and applying the amounts members designate to be deposited automatically into their accounts from their payroll checks. Correctly completed payroll deduction forms are critical. Incorrect forms are a serious source of error in deductions, and, when errors are made, members understandably become angry.

Your job is not only to provide payroll deduction forms to members, but also to explain *how* to complete them and to verify members' wishes once the forms are returned. If a member is paid twice a month and requests that $150 go into a share account, for example, verify that the member wants $150 to go in *each* payday, not once a month. In addition, you may need to direct the member to the appropriate department in your credit union for further assistance.

> *The loan department is fundamental, because the interest members pay on loans supports the credit union.*

The **loan department** is fundamental, because the interest members pay on loans supports the credit union. Employees in the loan department are responsible for taking and processing credit applications, submitting them for decisions, informing members of those decisions, setting up approved loans on the computer, processing the necessary documents, and closing loans. Credit unions may offer credit cards, consumer loans, vehicle loans, home equity loans and lines of credit, and mortgages.

Any member of the credit union is eligible to apply for a loan. The **credit committee,** or authorized loan officers, decide whether to approve a loan application based on policies established by the board of directors, and on state and federal laws and regulations. Depending on your credit union's policies, you may support the work of the loan department when providing loan applications to members, establishing new loans, posting loan payments, paying off loans, and informing members about loan promotions and special offers.

Investment services at each credit union vary, but an **investment department** may offer share certificates, money market accounts, and individual retirement accounts (IRAs). All of these accounts earn higher dividends than regular share accounts because they may require minimum balances, minimum time on deposit, and/or limitations on the number of withdrawals. IRAs are special savings accounts regulated by federal tax law. Some credit unions also offer financial planning and stock market investment services to their members in partnership with a brokerage. Your job as a teller is to know your credit union's requirements for these accounts and to remind members that their withdrawal requests may create a dividend penalty or fee.

The **information services (IS) department** maintains the computer hardware and software your credit union uses for record keeping and member service. You probably use a computer to process member transactions. The data you enter is used by other departments/functions to maintain up-to-date member records and provide reliable service. Some credit unions have automated processes, such as qualifying loan applications, that were once handled manually. IS staff members also maintain phone center routing systems and online account access services offered through the World Wide Web. They may provide computer training for credit union employees and help you respond to inquiries from members about automated services or problems with their accounts. Find out how your credit union uses technology to better serve members and know whom to contact when members have questions about those services.

Initially, it may seem the **collections department** has no connection to tellers or member service representatives because it is responsible for contacting members who are slow in repaying their loans. In some cases, collections employees may need your help to recover the credit union's money. As part of the original loan agreement, for example, credit unions usually include the right to access any funds in members' share accounts if they become past due on their payments. Collections employees can request a hold on those funds or transfer them as payment for the loan. However, members may come to the teller window and ask to withdraw those funds. In such cases, your computer will probably show a message explaining why the hold exists. If that happens, don't override the hold or embarrass the member by publicly announcing why the funds are unavailable. You may want to inform the member quietly that a hold exists and that you will get someone to explain it. It is your job to know the credit union's collection policies, your part in carrying out those policies, and members' rights to their funds.

Another credit union department is **human resources (HR),** which handles your employee records, payroll, and benefits at the credit union. The HR department also may be responsible for recruiting and training credit union employees. Your responsibility is to notify human resources staff promptly whenever information on your records changes, such as your address, home phone, or life insurance beneficiary. You are also responsible to provide any required documents, such as time records, doctor's statements of illness, or vacation requests, promptly and according to policy. Whenever you aren't sure of what is required, make sure you ask questions.

The **marketing department** develops promotions for the credit union. It encourages members to use additional services by advertising these services through the mail; on the radio, television, or Internet; in publications; and at the credit union itself. It may also educate members with periodic newsletters. Though some employees work exclusively on promoting products and services, marketing is everyone's responsibility at the credit union. Providing good member service is a central goal of marketing. In addition, you will assist the marketing department by reminding members about special promotions and suggesting products and services that will save them time and money.

To learn more about other credit union departments, ask your supervisor. Find out if you can observe operations in other departments before your counter opens or during slow times of day. See if your credit union has any training videos, computer programs, or books describing what each department does. Ask if you can read the procedures manual for different departments. If other tellers are interested, check the possibility of having someone from another department attend a teller meeting and answer your questions. No matter which option you choose, your supervisor will appreciate your desire to learn more.

Your Role in Relation to Management

In addition to relationships with members and other departments, tellers have an important relationship with credit union managers.

Support Policies and Procedures

An important responsibility you have to management is following the policies established by your credit union's board of directors and management. **Policies** are guidelines that direct credit union operations. The board of directors establishes policies to ensure compliance with federal and state laws, consistency in dealing with accounts, efficiency of service, and limitation of the credit union's risk.

You are also responsible for following procedures. **Procedures** are step-by-step methods for handling important operations, such as opening accounts, closing accounts, and making withdrawals. The credit union probably has a procedure for every duty you perform. Procedures are established for four important reasons:

- They ensure consistency.
- They promote accuracy.
- They specify actions needed to adhere to credit union policies.
- They establish standards for smoother, more efficient member service.

Your job as teller is to follow credit union policies and procedures consistently. If you don't agree with a procedure or don't understand why it is required, ask your supervisor. If you think you have a better idea, suggest it to management. You may have come up with a new, more efficient process. But unless your suggestion is formally adopted, stick to standard procedures. Some procedures are required by law; your credit union could face legal action if you do not follow them. Some are designed to prevent fraud. Other procedures make it easier for people to work together as a group and for departments to interact with one another.

Represent Members to Management

Your responsibility to management also involves representing members' concerns. Because you have the most direct contact with members, you will frequently hear members' concerns and opinions about credit union services. For example, members may particularly like a certain service or dislike a certain policy. It is up to you to convey these comments to management. Tellers are the eyes and ears of the credit union. An important part of your job is to communicate information to the rest of the team.

Represent Management to Members

When changes occur, make sure you have a solid understanding of what the change means for your job and how it affects members.

In the reverse, you are also an important representative of management to members. When changes occur, make sure you have a solid understanding of what the change means for your job and how it affects members. Then, you will be better able to explain the change to members and support it. For example, the cost of a certain fee may have been increased. As much as credit unions try to keep fees low, occasionally an increase is necessary. It's part of your job to explain these changes politely to members and, although it's understandable that members do not like cost increases, it's important that you support the change.

Show your support of management by saying "we" rather than "they" as you explain changes. For example, you might say, "Unfortunately, we needed to increase the fee because our costs for the service had increased." This is more effective than saying, "They had to increase the fee because they found that their costs for the service had increased." By using "we" rather than "they," you are speaking for the credit union and are a credible source of the information. Saying "they" makes you sound like you do not support the change and take no responsibility for implementing it. As the ambassador to members, you are the interpreter and representative for credit union policies.

In summary, your credit union is different from any other financial institution and different from any other credit union. It has a unique history, philosophy, and organization—and it is depending on you to carry on the tradition. To do so, you must thoroughly understand the "people helping people" philosophy and the way your credit union adheres to that standard. Your credit union is counting on you to use that philosophy to guide every interaction you have with members.

CHECK IT OUT! ✔

Your Knowledge of How Your Credit Union Is Organized

Directions: Find out and write down the answers to the questions below.

What is your credit union's field of membership?

Is it community-based? If so, what area does it include?

Does it include different employer groups? If so, list them below or obtain a list.

When is your credit union's annual meeting? Where is it held?

Your Knowledge of Members

Directions: In your credit union, what are four specific ways you can fulfill each of the teller roles listed below?

A.   You are an ambassador when you

1.

2.

3.

4.

B.   You are a teacher when you

1.

2.

3.

4.

C.   You are a service provider when you

1.

2.

3.

4.

Now discuss your answers with your supervisor. Write any additional ideas the
two of you share.

_____   _____
Your Signature   Supervisor's Signature

_____   _____
Date   Date

Your Knowledge of Other Departments

Directions: For each credit union department/function listed, rate yourself on how knowledgeable you are about what it does and how it operates. List any additional departments that are not shown.

Department	Ratings				
	Well-Informed			Not Informed	
1. Accounting	5	4	3	2	1
2. Share draft	5	4	3	2	1
3. Payroll deduction	5	4	3	2	1
4. Loans	5	4	3	2	1
5. Investments	5	4	3	2	1
6. Information services	5	4	3	2	1
7. Collections	5	4	3	2	1
8. Human resources	5	4	3	2	1
9. Marketing	5	4	3	2	1
10. _____	5	4	3	2	1
11. _____	5	4	3	2	1
12. _____	5	4	3	2	1

Department to Research	Contact Person
1.	
2.	
3.	

For any department you rated a 3 or less, find out who can help you learn more. Discuss your need with your supervisor, and set a date by which you can accomplish your goal.

Your Knowledge of Management

Directions: Who are the members of management and the board of directors? Find out the names of the managers and board members you are likely to meet and list them below.

Name:

Title:

Name:

Title:

Name:

Title:

Name:

Title:

Name:

Title:

Name:

Title:

CREDIT UNION PRODUCTS AND SERVICES

Here's a Tall Story From . . .

. . . an old Saturday Night Live *skit. It opens with a view in front of* The Change Bank's *pillars . . . then takes us to the teller line. There we find a paunchy, visor-clad male banker, and we listen for the pitch.*

"Afternoon. Step right up. What can I help you with? I think you'll find us up to the task . . . We here at The Change Bank *pride ourselves in finding creative solutions to customer problems. Skeptical, huh? Got a minute?*

"Let me tell you. Last week a fella came in here with a twenty. Needed to know his options. Took me only a second. 'Will that be two tens, a ten and two fives, four fives or maybe twenty ones?' Blew him away. He had so many choices on his hands he didn't know what to do . . . had me write them down so he could think them over.

"Then yesterday, this gorgeous lady comes in with a ten spot. Says she needs advice. 'I've got your answers,' I tell her. 'How about two fives, or a five and five ones, or ten ones?' Then just to show off a bit I say, 'Or how about forty quarters?' Earned myself a dinner date on that one.

"So as you can see, we know our business here at The Change Bank *. . . it's making change . . . that's all we do."*

Unlike *The Change Bank,* your credit union offers a great variety of financial products and services. Credit unions range in size from less than one million dollars in assets and a few hundred members to billion dollar institutions providing many thousands of members with a wide range of services. Which services and how many depend on the size of the credit union and the needs of its members. Generally speaking, credit unions offer the same consumer services as banks and other financial institutions. The difference is that savings rates are usually higher, while loan rates and fees are usually lower. Credit unions also emphasize educating members about their finances. Figure 2.1 lists the range of services that a credit union may offer.

Not surprisingly, as you are the focal point for many members' interaction with the credit union, you're involved with the full range of services your credit union offers. You may have specific job duties relating to certain services, or you may need to refer members to other employees for help with other services.

Stay informed about *all* the services available to members so you can connect them with services they may need. For example, your credit union may offer members lower fees on share draft accounts than they are paying now on checking accounts held with banks. Members shopping for a new car may not know your credit union offers an online auto buying service at no cost. Some members may think of your credit union only as the place where they keep their savings account. By informing them about other valuable services, you can save them time and money. To do so, you must keep up with changes in the financial field and know what other institutions are doing. You can also serve members by relaying their suggestions to management about what new products the credit union should offer or how it can improve its services.

Let's review the typical services credit unions offer. Learning about these services will give you a basic grounding in both your credit union's services and the competition. Find out which of these services your credit union offers and what your responsibilities are in providing these services to members.

SAVINGS

Credit unions offer similar types of savings and checking accounts as many other financial institutions, but terminology and features may differ. For instance,

Figure 2.1 Typical Credit Union Services

Savings	Convenience Services
• Share accounts • Share drafts • Share certificates • Money market accounts • Individual retirement accounts • Christmas clubs • Vacation clubs	• Direct deposit • Payroll deduction • Debit cards • Automatic teller machines • Call centers (account inquiries, transfers, loan-by-phone) • Online branches (PC account access, share draft ordering, loan applications and calculators) • Automated branches and kiosks • Bill-paying service • Drive-through tellers • Night depositories
Loans	**Other Services**
• Personal loans • Vehicle loans (direct and indirect) • Credit cards • Mortgages • Home equity loans • Home improvement loans • Lines of credit • Overdraft protection loans • Business loans • Student loans	• Member education • Credit counseling • Traveler's checks • Money orders • Wire transfers • Safe deposit boxes • Auto quote or buying service • Financial planning • Insurance services

what banks refer to as *checking accounts,* many credit unions call *share draft accounts.* Your most frequent responsibilities for these accounts will be opening accounts, processing deposits and withdrawals, closing accounts, and answering members' questions. Members may ask you to verify if a certain draft has cleared the account or what the balance is. You will also cash drafts that members write against their accounts.

Regular Share (Saving) Accounts

Credit union shares represent the "share" of the credit union owned by a member.

Credit unions offer regular **share accounts,** which are similar to savings accounts in other financial institutions. Credit union shares, however, represent the amount of money a person deposits to become a member in a credit union. This amount represents the "share" of the credit union owned by a member, and the member's shares earn dividends. In general, regular share accounts have a minimum balance requirement to earn dividends. Members can deposit or withdraw any amount, but they must maintain a share account to be credit union members. Dividends may be added to share accounts on a quarterly or monthly basis.

Members use these accounts for short-term savings goals, such as building up an emergency nest egg or saving for a vacation or major purchase. Regular share accounts are often the first savings account that a member opens.

Share Draft (Checking) Accounts

Credit unions also offer **share draft,** or **share checking, accounts,** which are comparable to checking accounts at other financial institutions. The term *share draft* refers to members debiting funds from share accounts by using a piece of paper, the *draft.* Although it has some differences, a share draft is similar to a check for most members' purposes. Share draft accounts may also earn dividends. Most credit unions reduce the cost to members of maintaining these accounts by "truncating," or safekeeping, the drafts members write. Members have a carbonless copy of the draft and can obtain a copy of the original if it is needed to prove payment.

Members use these accounts for daily bill-paying and other needs that are easiest to fulfill by writing a draft. These accounts give members the freedom to access funds in their accounts without having to come into the credit union office.

Share Certificates (Certificate Accounts)

Share certificates are accounts requiring a minimum length of time that the funds must remain in the account. Usually, if the member withdraws the funds before the minimum time, or *term,* is completed, a monetary penalty, such as loss of dividends, is assessed. The certificates have a variety of terms available, such as 6-month, 12-month, 24-month, or even longer. These accounts often require a higher minimum balance than regular share or share draft accounts.

Members use these accounts when saving for longer-term financial goals, such as saving for retirement or a child's education. They are also useful ways to save money that is received in a large lump sum, such as an inheritance.

Other Accounts

Credit unions may offer some or all of the following accounts:

- *Money market accounts:* high-yield accounts that usually require a high minimum balance but give greater flexibility in accessing the funds than certificates do.
- *Individual retirement accounts (IRAs):* savings plans with tax-deferred benefits. Wage earners put aside part of their earnings for their retirement while deferring federal income taxes. Congress has created several different types of IRAs, including accounts to save for children's education, all with specific rules and restrictions.
- *Special purpose accounts:* accounts that help members save for a specific purpose such as holiday spending or vacations. Some credit unions have a generic special purpose account in which the member selects the savings goal and designates the account for that purpose.

LOANS

Credit unions use member funds in share accounts to make loans to members. Loans are the most fundamental expression of how the cooperative aspect of credit unions works. Some members have excess funds to put into share accounts and other members need to borrow money. The credit union brings the needs of these members together for mutual benefit. Members who get loans pay *interest* for the use of the money, and members who put their funds in share accounts receive *dividends.* All of them fulfill their financial goals.

> *Members who get loans pay* **interest** *for the use of the money, and members who put their funds in share accounts receive* **dividends.** *All of them fulfill their financial goals.*

Your involvement with the loans and other credit services of your credit union will usually be through accepting and crediting payments, responding to member inquiries about loan and credit card balances, and promoting special offers on loans that can save members money.

Auto Loans

Whether a member drives a car, truck, mini-van, or motorcycle, odds are he or she will need a loan to purchase a vehicle. Credit unions make a high volume of these loans and often help members with the shopping and car-buying process. These loans are approved based on members' creditworthiness and the pledge of the car as **collateral** (security) for the loan.

Personal Loans

Personal loans are usually short-term loans granted based on the member's creditworthiness. No collateral secures these loans so they are sometimes called *signature loans.* Personal loans can be used for almost any purpose; credit unions sometimes sponsor special promotions for personal loans to be used for vacations, computer purchases, or tax payments.

Residential Real Estate Loans

Large credit unions may offer loans for members to purchase homes. These long-term loans, called **mortgages,** typically are repaid over ten to thirty years; the home is the collateral. When mortgage interest rates decrease, many homeowners refinance their home loans to reduce their monthly payments. In recent years, credit union mortgage loan officers have been as busy with **refinancing** as they have been processing mortgages to purchase homes.

Home ownership is a common goal for members and represents a significant achievement and source of pride. A more tangible benefit is that members with residential real estate loans can usually take advantage of a federal income tax deduction for loan interest.

Whether or not they offer mortgages, many credit unions offer **home equity loans** or lines of credit, which use the portion of a member's home value not covered by a mortgage (the equity) as collateral. Members can use the loan proceeds for home improvements or other purposes.

Here's an example: The Chan family owns a home valued at $140,000, and they owe $75,000 on their mortgage. Thus, they have an equity interest of $65,000 in their home. When the Chans decide to remodel their kitchen, they can borrow against their equity, up to a certain percentage of the home's value. Because they are secured by collateral, home equity loans are usually offered at lower interest rates than personal loans. Another advantage is that members may be able to deduct interest paid on home equity loans from federal taxes.

Credit Cards

A **credit card** represents a *line of credit* or approved maximum amount of money that the member can borrow over a future period. A member uses a credit card to purchase goods and services wherever the card is accepted. Every month, the member is billed for the balance outstanding in the line of credit. Many members make a partial payment each month and pay off their purchases gradually. In a way, you could say that the member gets an "instant" loan when he or she uses a credit card.

Other Loans and Credit Services

Following are other types of loans and credit services that your credit union may offer.

- *Business loans:* Many community-based credit unions make business loans to members. These loans can be used to start a business, finance an expansion, or purchase equipment.
- *Overdraft protection:* Another form of credit helps members who may accidentally overdraw their share draft accounts. Occasionally, members may make an error and think they have more funds than they actually do in the account. To avoid having a share draft returned for insufficient funds, some members apply for overdraft protection. This is similar to a line of credit that is activated if the debit of a share draft would bring an account below a zero balance. Overdraft protection means the share draft is paid, and the member pays interest for the time the funds are "lent" to the member.
- *Credit life and disability insurance:* Your credit union may offer borrowers low-cost insurance that pays off loans and credit card balances if the member dies or makes loan payments while a member is disabled.

CONVENIENCE SERVICES

Beyond savings accounts, share drafts, and loans, credit unions offer a variety of services designed to save members time and make handling their financial needs easier. Many are offered at no or low cost, but they are so valued that some members choose your credit union as their primary financial institution largely because of these convenience services. You can help members by making sure they are aware these services are available.

Direct deposit and payroll deductions are two popular convenience services. Members use **direct deposit** to authorize their employers to deposit paychecks directly to their credit union accounts; Social Security, retirement checks, and other payments may also be deposited directly. Members can authorize **payroll deductions** to pay credit union loans directly from their paychecks or to deposit a portion of their paychecks to savings, IRA, or other accounts. You will need to supply members with the proper authorization forms for these services.

Debit cards are relatively new, offering a convenient alternative to writing share drafts for purchases. Debit cards look like credit cards but act like share drafts. When members use debit cards, the purchase amount is deducted from their share draft, or checking, account.

Automated services represent a new and expanding area of convenience for members. The chief advantage of these options is that they are available to members beyond the regular hours that credit union branches are open. In fact, some of these delivery channels are available 24 hours a day, seven days a week.

Automated teller machines (ATMs) are the most common example of using technology to serve members. Some credit unions also maintain kiosks and automated branches, which provide services beyond those offered at a typical ATM, such as account access and loan applications. Many larger credit unions operate call centers for members who prefer to conduct financial transactions by phone; in addition, some credit unions offer 24-hour, automated phone services so members can access their accounts by using phone keypads.

Online branches are the most recent innovation in financial services. Members can use personal computers at work and at home to obtain access to their accounts via the Internet or a direct-dial link to the credit union computer. Online branches may offer these services:

- account access so members can check balances or make other inquiries
- transfers between accounts
- electronic histories members can download to balance accounts
- share draft ordering
- loan applications and interest and payment calculators
- bill-paying services members can use to automate payments to creditors, utilities, etc.
- auto-buying services
- e-mail links to credit union staff to report problems or ask questions

Your contact with members who regularly use electronic services may be limited because they have little reason to visit your branch. But you should be familiar with these services so you can assist members who have questions about them. Some of those questions may be technical, so find out which credit union employee can help members with those inquiries.

Other examples of convenience services include drive-through tellers and night depositories. They may not be high-tech, but many members value these time-saving options.

OTHER SERVICES

Credit unions offer seminars on topics such as managing personal finances, budgeting, developing saving habits, purchasing cars and other major items wisely, and qualifying for loans.

The quality and quantity of **member education** sets credit unions apart from their competitors. Many credit unions offer seminars on topics such as managing personal finances, budgeting, developing saving habits, purchasing cars and other major items wisely, and qualifying for loans. Other forms of member education may include

- regular member newsletters on credit union services and personal finances
- web sites featuring how-to articles, FAQs (frequently asked questions), worksheets, and calculators on retirement savings, home buying, vehicle purchases, and other topics
- a library of money management books available to members at the credit union office
- opportunities to join buying clubs or use purchase discounts

In addition, many credit union employees informally help members who are new to using share accounts and lending services. Because credit unions want their members to be successful at managing their money, they are committed to making education and resources available.

Credit counseling is another valuable form of member education. Sometimes credit union members who have loans or credit cards may find that, due to temporary setbacks such as illnesses or job loss, they are having difficulty meeting their payments. Or, some members may be less experienced with handling debt and become over-committed. Other types of financial institutions are less likely to work with these members to the extent that credit unions will. Many credit unions offer both formal and informal credit counseling for overextended borrowers. Of course, credit unions must protect the funds that other members have entrusted to the credit union for lending purposes. But credit unions will try harder to help overextended borrowers get back in control of their finances. In some cases, credit unions may offer a loan consolidation option, so that members can combine loan and credit card balances into one loan to lower the number and amount of required monthly payments.

To provide "one-stop shopping" for financial services, some credit unions have begun to offer **financial planning** and counseling and insurance services. In many cases those services are offered in partnership with a specialized insurance or investment firm. Access to auto quote or buying services, particularly those offered over the Internet, are also becoming increasingly common benefits of credit union membership.

Other services that credit unions may offer include traveler's checks, money orders, wire transfers, and safe deposit boxes. Some of those services will be offered at the teller window, so you will need to learn how to complete those transactions.

As you can see from this variety of services, your credit union is dedicated to helping members manage their finances as profitably and efficiently as possible. Your responsibility toward this end is crucial. Members depend on you not only for courteous and accurate service but also for information about the full range of services your credit union offers.

CHECK IT OUT! ✔

Your Credit Union's Services

Directions: Obtain brochures about your credit union services and compare the descriptions to the products and services listed in the chapter. Also, talk to co-workers and supervisors to find out more about your credit union's services.

Put a check mark by the services below that your credit union offers and add to the list any others that your credit union offers.

_____ Regular share (savings) accounts

_____ Share draft (checking) accounts

_____ Share certificates

_____ Money market accounts

_____ Individual retirement accounts (IRAs)

_____ Special purpose accounts (holiday, vacation, etc.)

_____ Auto loans

_____ Personal (signature) loans

_____ Residential real estate loans (mortgages)

_____ Credit cards

_____ Home equity loans (or lines of credit)

_____ Business loans

_____ Overdraft protection

_____ Credit life and disability insurance

_____ Money management seminars

_____ Member education (newsletter/magazine)

_____ Credit counseling

_____ ATMs (automated teller machines)

_____ Direct deposit

_____ Payroll deduction

_____ Automated telephone access

_____ Automatic loan payments

_____ Online branch

_____ Bill-paying service

_____ Debit cards

_____ Check guarantee cards

_____ Drive-up window service

_____ Night depository

_____ Safe deposit boxes

_____ Traveler's checks

_____ Gift checks

_____ Money orders

_____ Cashiers checks

_____ Copy service

_____ Notary service

_____ Telephone transfers and payments

_____ Children's club

_____ Coin counting

_____ Senior citizen club

_____ Wire transfers

_____ Auto quote or buying service

_____ Financial planning

_____ Insurance services

_____ _____

_____ _____

RELATING TO MEMBERS

Here is a simple but powerful rule: always give people more than they expect to get.

—*Nelson Boswell*

Be everywhere, do everything, and never fail to astonish the customer.

—*Macy's motto*

These quotes (and others you'll see in this chapter) have one thing in common. They all relate to different aspects of quality member service. Quality service is the primary goal of any financial institution. But because of our unique history, credit unions strive to provide an even higher level of service. Achieving that level depends most importantly on the member service you give as a teller.

Yours is a people job. Working as a teller requires attention to detail, accuracy, and a thorough understanding of credit union products and procedures. But success as a front-line credit union employee requires that you enjoy working with people. A friendly, courteous attitude is as critical as any money-handling skill.

A key ingredient in effective member relations is communication. Communicating effectively is often taken for granted. Too frequently, people assume they are expert communicators because they have been communicating since birth. Unfortunately, this is not true. Communication is a two-way process in which information is exchanged and understood. It is necessary not only to speak, but to listen carefully and make sure you understand what members are saying. Have you ever ordered a catalog item by telephone, but received the wrong merchandise? You talked, the employee thought he or she listened, but no effective communication occurred. Something else was needed. In this chapter, you'll read about techniques that can help you improve your communication skills and relationships with members.

GENERAL GUIDELINES FOR QUALITY MEMBER SERVICE

In all situations when you are working with members, the following six guidelines will help you deliver excellent service (see figure 3.1).

Be Courteous

Being courteous is the most effective technique you can develop when serving members. It doesn't take elaborate training—just a continual desire to treat people with respect and good manners.

Picture yourself in a restaurant, ready to order. The waitress quickly appears. Instead of greeting you, she simply asks for your order. When the food arrives, you discover that you do not have a fork, so you ask for one. She promptly gives it to you, but with no smile or apology. During your meal, she returns once to solemnly ask if you need anything. Then she disappears until the moment you take your last bite. Immediately, she whisks away your plate and hands you the check. You pay for the meal, but leave a minimal tip. The service was prompt, but it was not courteous. Rather than treating you like an individual, the waitress acted as if you were just one more duty to perform.

Figure 3.1 Guidelines for Quality Member Service

- Be courteous.
- Be friendly, but maintain professionalism.
- Use tact.
- Maintain confidentiality.
- Avoid jargon.
- Be organized and prepared to serve members.

Contrast that description with this situation. You and a friend go to your favorite restaurant and are seated with the usual efficiency and pleasant manners. Your waiter takes your orders and you relax over bread and beverages. Soon, he's back with your orders, and you prepare to enjoy the meal.

Everything seems all right but after he leaves, your friend realizes that her food is not prepared the way she ordered (she asked for "no cheese" because she is allergic to it). You signal the waiter and he comes over to your table. You tell him the problem and he immediately apologizes and says he will have the correct order in just a few minutes. When he delivers the order, he apologizes again and waits until your friend can see that there is no cheese in her food. You thank him and he says, "Hey, it was our fault. I'm really sorry you had to wait longer." He comes back later to double-check that everything else is all right. When he brings your check, he thanks you and says he hopes you'll come back again. He emphasizes that the cooks are usually very accurate with the orders so you should expect good service. For this waiter, you leave a good tip and remark to your friend on how the waiter really tried to make up for the mistake.

In this situation, even though the mistake was bigger, the waiter's courteous efforts to overcome the problem more than compensated for it. Simple courtesy made the difference.

Members react in a similar way. Instead of tipping, they respond to your service by either returning to the credit union or not. When you are courteous, you show you care about members as individuals and demonstrate that you'll be happy to help them whenever they return.

As you can see in the restaurant example, you show simple courtesy by saying "please" and "thank you." Deliver sincere apologies for errors. Whether or not you are responsible for the error, saying "I'm sorry" can go a long way to settling down an angry member.

Be Friendly

Friendliness always personalizes a relationship. It demonstrates your desire to treat a member as an individual, not a number. It means remembering their names, asking about recent trips they may have taken or family members they have mentioned, complimenting them on new outfits or hairstyles, and chatting about the weather. But friendliness has limits in the member relations setting. Avoid trying to become too close by discussing topics that are too personal or intrusive. For example, don't teasingly criticize a member, even in a joking way. And don't make jokes about transactions, such as commenting to a member making a large deposit, "You must have gotten a windfall!"

Use Tact

Tact is, after all, a kind of mind-reading.

—Sarah Orne Jewett

Tact is also part of maintaining good relationships with members. Tact means the ability to choose your words in a way that does not annoy or offend someone. Tact is particularly important when members make errors or you are unable to fulfill what they want because of a credit union policy. Remind members gently of your credit union's policies. Choose your words diplomatically and seek to create a cordial environment instead of bluntly stating a policy or saying they can't do something. For instance, if a member hands you a cash withdrawal slip without a signature, think how she would react if you said, "I can't give you the cash without your signature." Instead, you could say, "Okay, Mrs. Sanchez, I'll get that for you. All I need is your signature right here." Being tactful is simply taking the time to polish what you say.

Maintain Confidentiality

Who could deny that privacy is a jewel?

—Phyllis McGinley

Maintaining confidentiality is another important technique to use for good member relationships. Members trust you with their money and with information about how they spend it. Most people are sensitive about who has information about their finances. Maintaining confidentiality is respectful of members' privacy.

Confidentiality takes many forms:

- When members request their balances, write down the numbers and show them rather than saying the amount. That way, your members' accounts remain private.
- Speak in a low tone of voice while you discuss their transactions or count cash.
- Never comment about someone else's business to another member.
- Discuss a member's transaction with other employees only when necessary.

At many credit unions, your members may also be your and other employees' neighbors, so minimizing discussion of their finances can be particularly important.

Avoid Jargon

Jargon refers to financial terms or special abbreviations that members may not understand. As long as it is used among coworkers, jargon is perfectly acceptable. However, using such terms with members may confuse them. Be careful not to use acronyms the member may not understand. For example, many members may know they need a PIN to access their accounts at an ATM, but don't assume they know those acronyms. If they don't understand, they may feel embarrassed because they feel ignorant and must ask you to explain the term. Or, they may pretend to understand and leave in confusion. Neither option helps build a good relationship.

If you ever wonder if a certain word is financial jargon, just ask yourself, "Where and when did I learn this word?" If the answers are "at the credit union" and "after I started working here," then it's likely that the term is financial jargon. See figure 3.2 for examples of financial jargon and more acceptable terms.

Be Prepared

Being prepared to help members allows you to serve them promptly, efficiently, and accurately. Keep the supplies and forms you need for most transactions within easy reach. If you must search for a pen every time a member comes to your window, you come across as disorganized. If you can't easily locate the forms needed in even the most commonplace transaction, members must wait as you track down what you need. Their positive attitude can quickly turn to impatience. Lack of preparation and disorganization increases the risk of making mistakes while processing a transaction.

Figure 3.2 Financial Jargon

If you use these terms . . .	Add these explanations:
ACH payment	"an electronic payment to or from another financial institution"
Accrued earnings	"dividends your account has earned that we haven't yet paid"
Annual percentage yield (APY)	"how much your account will earn over a year, when dividends are compounded"
Check digit	"the last digit that appears in your account number on your share drafts or checks; it's calculated using your account number, so it verifies that your account number is printed correctly"
Collected funds	"money we aren't waiting to receive from other financial institutions for checks or other items you deposited"
Debit card	"it works like an electronic share draft (or check)"
Dividend	"the earnings on your accounts; we call them dividends rather than interest because the earnings are your return for being an owner of the credit union"
Dormant account	"an account you haven't used for ___ months or more"
Early withdrawal penalty	"an amount you would pay for withdrawing funds from this account before it matures"
Exception item	"a transaction that can't be processed the usual way because..."
Float	"the time it takes a check to clear"
Funds availability	"the amount of your money that's available for withdrawal"
Garnishment	"legal action by a creditor to take repayment directly from a paycheck"

Figure 3.2 Financial Jargon (*continued*)

If you use these terms . . .	Add these explanations:
Maturity date	"the date on which your share certificate becomes available with all dividends paid"
Negotiable instrument	"cash or a share draft, traveler's check, bond, or other items that can be easily redeemed for cash"
PIN	"personal identification number"
Points	"a fee based on a set percentage on the loan amount, paid when the loan is made"
Postdated check	"dated later than today"
Power of attorney	"a legal document granting someone authority to conduct your financial affairs"
Promissory note	"the loan contract"
Remitter	"the person paying the funds"
Share draft	"some financial institutions call it a check"
Signature loan	"a loan not secured by collateral"
Smart card	"like a credit card but worth a set amount of money; it electronically counts down as its value is spent"
Stale-dated check	"a check dated more than ___ months previously, which can no longer be honored"
T-bill	"a short-term U.S. Treasury security"
Term	"the period of time over which you agree to repay this loan"
Tiered rate	"your account (or loan or credit card) may have different rates applied to it depending on…"
Transit number	"our electronic address for the check clearing system; also called a routing number or ABA number"

THE MEMBER RELATIONS PROCESS

When a member comes to your window, you can follow the process outlined in figure 3.3. This process works effectively in most situations.

Establish Eye Contact

Never try to look into both eyes at the same time. . . .
Switch your gaze from one eye to the other. That signals
warmth and sincerity.

—Dorothy Sarnoff

Eye contact is one of the most powerful signs of good communication. When you establish eye contact, you tell someone that you recognize that person as an individual rather than just another transaction. You also show that your complete attention is focused on the speaker. The member relations process should always begin with eye contact between you and the member.

It is helpful to make eye contact even before members step up to your window. If members wait in one line in your lobby for the next available teller, you can signal that you are ready to help them simply by making eye contact. Glancing at

Figure 3.3 The Member Relations Process

- Establish eye contact.
- Smile.
- Greet the member.
- Use the member's name.
- Listen actively.
- Promote additional services.
- Close pleasantly.

people waiting in line behind the member at your window acknowledges that you are aware they need service and signals that you will be with them shortly.

Smile

Another powerful form of nonverbal communication is *smiling*. More than anything else, a smile demonstrates friendliness and interest in the other person. It breaks the ice as a relationship begins, and it continues to set a positive tone. The simple act of smiling makes your voice more pleasant and your mannerisms more courteous. Take the initiative and smile at members as they approach your window.

Greet the Member

The initial contact with a member includes eye contact, a smile, and a *greeting*. Depending on your personal style, your greeting could be, "May I help you?" or "Good morning, how can I help you?" Do you know why you should always greet members rather than waiting for them to tell you what they want? In addition to being courteous, you establish several other important points. Your question establishes that you are in control of the situation and confident in your skills. You have focused your attention on the member and let the member know that you are now listening to him or her. The member will quickly get to the point of the visit and save time for both of you.

Many tellers establish a regular pattern to their greeting by smiling and saying similar words each time. This doesn't turn you into a robot. The reason for a standard greeting is that you will consistently approach members in a pleasant way even if it's a busy day or you face other pressures. Your job is easier because you know your good habits will come to your rescue even if you are a little distracted.

Use the Member's Name

The technique that transforms any basic interaction into a personal relationship is *using the person's name*. The impact is similar to receiving a personal invitation rather than a form letter. It shows that you see this person as a special individual rather than a faceless transaction. People are flattered that you bother to use their names and they will be more likely to respond positively to you. And, you never know if you'll need that member's goodwill later. What if you have to tell a member that a certain transaction will have a fee (bad news for any member!) or that you are unable to grant a request due to a policy? If you have already established a positive relationship with that member, you are more likely to defuse a potentially angry situation. The member will be more likely to recognize that you are just doing your job.

If you don't know a member's name, look on the deposit slip, membership card, or driver's license when it is presented to you. And don't be put off by names you don't know how to pronounce. Just ask! Again, most people are flattered that you are interested enough to ask. Most people don't mind if you say, "Is your name pronounced . . . ?"

Listen Actively

Listening actively is another effective communications technique. Active listening channels your attention to the speaker's content. Here's how to involve yourself in the member's message:

- Concentrate completely on what is said. Mentally shut out noises or other activities around you.
- Use short responses, such as "Oh," or "I see," which show you understand and are encouraging the person to talk.
- Use appropriate body language, such as nodding your head and looking at the member's face.
- Paraphrase what the person said to make sure you understand. For example, if the member has made a somewhat complicated request, you would want to verify by saying, "OK, Mr. Elston, let me make sure I've got this right. You'd like to deposit $300 of this check and get $50 back in a money order. Then, you'd also like some information on our credit cards, right?"

Active listening establishes an "I'm here to help" atmosphere. It pays the added dividend of helping you to concentrate on the transaction at hand, so you can complete it efficiently and accurately.

Promote Additional Services

Nothing great was ever achieved without enthusiasm.

—Ralph Waldo Emerson

Your first priority with all members is to help them accomplish the transactions they came to your office to conduct. In addition, you can help members make further use of your credit union's services—and save time and money. Here are some examples of how you can let members know about credit union products and services in a helpful way:

- Find ways that using other services can solve a member's problem. For example, a member might announce with a sigh that she's here, again, to make a loan payment. You might respond, "Well, I enjoy serving you every month, Mrs. Washington, but did you know we can automatically transfer that loan payment from your share draft account to save you this trip?"

- Look for and find clues to services that could help members better manage their finances. As his daughter tugs at his knee, a member might say ruefully, "She'll be grown up and heading for college before I know it—if we can afford college, that is." You could answer, "Have you heard about the accounts we offer for educational IRAs, a tax-free way to save for her college tuition? I have a brochure right here."

- Make sure members are aware of promotional offers and special rates. As a member completes a transaction, you could say, "And here's a complementary mouse pad that features the Web address of our new, convenient online branch. You can find out how easy it is to use on the demonstration kiosk in our lobby."

Some people may protest, "I'm a teller, not a marketing person." But your foremost job as teller is to serve members, and making sure they are aware of valuable credit union services and products helps members in three immediate ways:

- They save money on the credit union's lower interest rates and earn more dividends on savings accounts than they might at other financial institutions.

- The "one-stop shopping" advantage of holding several accounts at the credit union saves them time.

- The credit union earns additional revenue by offering more products, which allows the credit union to hold down interest rates and pay higher dividends to all members.

Close Pleasantly

The final communication skill is *closing pleasantly.* It is important to finish the interaction in a positive manner. First, you may want to summarize the transactions if you have handled several for the member. This will ensure that all the member's requests have been completed. Then, give the member an opportunity to add any final requests. For example, you could ask, "Is there anything else I can help you with today?" End your interaction with the member the same way you started it—with eye contact, a smile, and the member's name. You can also make a conversational close such as, "Have a good day" or whatever else is natural and appropriate for you and the member.

SPECIAL SITUATIONS

The techniques described above are a good general process, but you may encounter many unique situations as you work with members. How you handle these situations affects your credit union's relationships with members. Figure 3.4 summarizes the suggestions that follow, and you can expect to receive additional information or training in this area from your supervisor.

Irate Members

One of the least pleasant aspects of your job is dealing with irate members. Members may become angry for any number of reasons. The teller may have made a mistake during a transaction. There may be a slow line at each window. The member may disagree with a policy, or an error may have appeared on the member's statement. Whatever the cause, such members demonstrate their displeasure in no uncertain terms, and that behavior naturally causes anxiety among tellers. Try to view such members as a challenge, not a threat. Then, use the techniques listed below.

First, *stay calm.* That's easier to say than do. Your mental reaction is likely to be either "Hey, don't yell at me, or I'll yell at you" or "Get me out of here—I don't want to deal with this." These reactions are often called the "fight or flight" instinct, a natural response to stressful situations. Your instinct is to want to defend yourself or get away from the situation. But neither of these reactions will solve a problem with an irate member. If you obey the "fight" instinct, you'll be more likely to get into an argument than solve the problem. If you obey the "flight" instinct, you won't argue with the member but you may not listen very well. You

Figure 3.4 How to Handle Special Situations

Irate Members
- Stay calm.
- Listen.
- Show understanding.
- Identify the problem.
- Solve the problem.
- Keep your mood positive.

Lines
- Stay calm; don't get flustered.
- Acknowledge waiting members.
- Stay pleasant.
- Thank members for their patience in waiting.
- Get backup help, if possible.
- Stay positive.

Drive-Through Windows
- Concentrate on personalizing your service.
- Clarify and verify information.
- Remember that members are in a hurry.
- Acknowledge members waiting in other lanes.
- Thank members for their patience in waiting.
- Know your credit union's procedures for unusual circumstances.

Policy Explanations and Exceptions
- Understand the policy.
- Keep explanations brief.
- Stress reasons.
- Offer options.
- Get approval for exceptions.

Children
- Look for ways to occupy children if they are restless.
- Compliment good behavior often.
- Reinforce positive actions.

Members with Disabilities
- Treat them with respect.
- Offer assistance, but wait for acceptance and instructions.
- Communicate directly and with appropriate methods.
- Be sensitive in your references to specific disabilities.
- Know your credit union's accessibility features.

Older Members
- Treat them with respect.
- If older members have disabilities, respond as you would to others with that disability.

New Members
- Explain transactions as you complete them.
- Emphasize advantages of credit union membership.
- Promote other products that might be of value.

are more likely to avoid eye contact and concentrate more on getting out of the situation than dealing with it. Try to get past these first reactions and move into a problem-solving mode in which you concentrate more on what you're doing than what you're feeling.

Second, *listen*. Members who are upset want to talk about the problem. Focus on what they say and do not interrupt. Many people think of listening as passive, a way to avoid taking immediate action. In reality, listening is an active step to make sure you understand what other people are saying and feeling. Only if you listen will you hear what solution might resolve the problem. If you jump in too quickly, members may become angrier because they feel you are not letting them have their say. Allow them to let off steam and use this opportunity to gather important information. Use eye contact and keep an intent and serious look on your face (rather than a negative or annoyed look). Listen for information rather than getting distracted by angry (and probably exaggerated) words. By allowing members to have their say, you will often find that they will at least give you a chance to respond.

Third, *show understanding*. Let them know you can identify with their situation. Say, "I can understand why you feel frustrated" or "I know how you feel." This personalizes the confrontation and demonstrates your willingness to help.

Fourth, *identify the problem*. Make sure you know exactly what has happened to cause the anger. Here is where listening pays off. Rephrase what you have heard to clarify it. For example, if a member is angry about a fee, you could say, "I understand how you feel. Until now, we didn't have a fee for money orders, and now we've started charging for them. On top of that, you don't have enough cash with you today to pay the fee."

Fifth, *solve the problem*. Depending on the situation, the solution may be simple or complex. For example, if you (or someone else in the credit union) made a mistake, an apology and quick action to fix it will often solve the problem. The member may still be a little angry, but courtesy and fast action will usually earn forgiveness. If you can't solve the problem, get your supervisor or someone else who can help. If you can't leave your window, call another employee, and take time to explain the situation so the member doesn't have to repeat it all again. Be prepared to get help, too, if you see that the member will only be satisfied by speaking to someone with more authority or if a member becomes abusive.

Sometimes your credit union's policies may prevent you from offering the solution the member wants. Tactfully explain the policy to the member and if possible, offer other options.

Sixth, *keep your mood positive.* During the encounter, try to control your facial expressions and tone of voice so that you present a neutral and courteous manner. This isn't easy but the more you are successful at controlling your reactions, the more successful you will be at controlling the situation.

Challenge yourself to prevent the member's anger from affecting you for the rest of the day. Don't let one episode spoil your service to other members or relations with coworkers. Sometimes it's appropriate to let off a little steam of your own with coworkers because they will be sympathetic to your situation. However, they will enjoy your company more if you can shake off your reactions and move on to the rest of the day. And, never, under any circumstances should you complain or blow off steam within hearing distance of members.

Lines

People forget how fast you did a job—but they remember how well you did it.

—Howard W. Newton

Another stressful part of the teller's job occurs when lines form at the window. At those times, the teller's first instinct is to speed up so members won't have to wait. While that intention is good, such a response can create problems. Speeding up changes the pace to which you are accustomed. That can throw you off, like a runner breaking stride. As a result, mistakes may be more likely. The best solution is to keep a quick but comfortable pace while using the following techniques to handle the line.

First, *stay calm;* don't get frustrated or nervous. Remind yourself that you can only help one member at a time, and each member deserves your complete and accurate service.

Next, *acknowledge the waiting members.* Look up from time to time, smile, and make a friendly comment. This lets them know you're aware that they are waiting.

Remember to *stay pleasant*. You may be busy, but now more than ever it's important to smile and greet each member. First, offer a quick apology for the wait, and thank members for their patience.

Get back-up help. If help is available, the best time to call for it is when you see the line forming. Find out your credit union's procedure ahead of time.

Overall, *stay positive*. Sometimes, no matter what you do, members who have been waiting get upset. By the end of the transaction, they still may not have calmed down. Apologize again for the wait, thank them for their business, and continue with a pleasant attitude to the next member. Doing so will set a positive tone for the remainder of the line.

Drive-Through Windows

When you work in the credit union's drive-through, you perform the same duties as a counter teller, but under unique circumstances. Your environment requires special techniques.

Concentrate on personal service. The glass wall or remote camera is a physical barrier between you and members. As a result, you must work harder to counteract the impersonal feeling this barrier creates. Add more expression to your voice. Look directly at members as you speak, even if they are in cars fifty feet away. Smile frequently.

Clarify and verify information. Because the microphone you use picks up exterior sounds and static, members are not easy to hear. Also, members can't see what you're doing, so they can't correct you until after the transaction. Therefore, be sure to speak clearly and repeat requests whenever you are uncertain.

Next, remember that people who use drive-throughs are in a hurry. Waiting in a car often seems longer than waiting at the counter, because people can't hear what is happening ahead of them. When a line forms, *work at your fastest comfortable pace*. If you are working two lanes, acknowledge the member in the other lane. Again, *thank the member for waiting*.

Finally, know your credit union's procedures for unusual circumstances. If, for example, a member remains in the drive-through, saying you sent an incorrect amount of cash back in the carrier, what would you do? Unlike the counter, you can't simply recount the money to verify the amount. You have no way of knowing whether or not the member replaced all the cash in the carrier if they returned it for recounting. Find out ahead of time how you should handle such situations.

Policy Explanations and Exceptions

One type of situation can come up at any time when you are helping members: explaining credit union policies and making exceptions. Sometimes members will question why a policy exists. They may be angry about a rule you are enforcing. Or, they may simply want clarification. At any rate, you should be able to explain credit union policies effectively to your members. To do so:

1. Understand the policies yourself. Ask questions if they don't make sense in an obvious way. You won't be able to explain what you don't understand.

2. Keep your explanation brief and clear. Don't cloud the issue with information that doesn't apply.

3. Stress reasons for the policy and the benefits to members. Show how the policy is designed to protect the best interests of all members. Never say, "that's our policy" without providing an explanation. Members will become even more annoyed if you don't consider their viewpoint or at least try to help them understand the credit union's reasons.

4. Offer options. If the policy prevents you from handling a member's request, suggest other ways to help the member. This can actually be an opportunity to promote other credit union services.

Occasionally some situations may require exceptions to policies and procedures. The key to successful handling of these situations is to know when you have the authority to make an exception. Otherwise, always obtain a supervisor's approval. Never override a policy on your own, if you are not certain you have the authority. If you feel an exception is warranted, consult someone who has the authority.

Children

Children who accompany their parents to the credit union provide an excellent topic of conversation with parents, who love to be complimented on their offspring. However, children are not always well mannered. When small children must wait in line, their patience disappears faster than that of their parents.

Your job is to help children behave and to keep their parents happy. If a small child waits at your window with his or her parent, you may want to make an occasional remark to the child such as asking his or her name or age. In this way, you will catch the child's attention and help prevent boredom. Your credit union may have a children's table or play corner where children can play while they wait. Or, if you distribute candy or balloons at your credit union, remember to do so at the beginning of the transaction instead of at the end. Be sure to get permission from the parent first.

When children themselves are members, you will need to be patient as they may take a little longer to complete transactions. If possible, show them how they can prepare ahead of time to proceed more quickly. Successfully handling children will strengthen your relationship with parents.

Members with Disabilities

The Americans with Disabilities Act (ADA) sets out specific rules and guidelines for making service accessible to individuals with disabilities. Doors that provide for wheelchair access and designated parking places are examples that you have probably seen at many businesses. You should find out the features of your credit union that specifically assist members with disabilities so you can tell phone callers or answer other questions.

A critical part of how you make your credit union's services accessible to members with disabilities is through your personal service. In general, the most important aspect of helping members with disabilities is to treat them with respect and remain sensitive to their needs.

Success in life has nothing to do with what you gain in life or accomplish for yourself. It's what you do for others.

—Danny Thomas

First, use common sense. Members with disabilities appreciate being treated the same as other members—with courtesy, friendliness, and consideration.

Feel free to offer assistance but always wait for the member to accept before taking action such as pushing a wheelchair or filling out forms. When you offer help, ask the member in what way you can help. Don't be the one to decide what help the member needs. If members would like help, they will tell you what they need. Otherwise, your help could be perceived as patronizing rather than simple courtesy.

Another point to remember is to talk or communicate directly with the member with the disability. Even if he or she is accompanied by a friend or relative, if the member is the person with the disability, then address your communication to that person. For example, you may need to write notes to a member with a hearing impairment.

Finally, whether you are working directly with members with disabilities or talking about their business (as needed) with your supervisor or other employees, you can take one other action that helps show your sensitivity and respect. Avoid certain words or phrases that have been commonly used in the past but either annoy members with disabilities or emphasize the disability rather than the person. For example, don't say a member is "deaf." He or she is "a person with a hearing impairment." Another example is "handicapped" or "crippled." Simply use words that specifically describe the disability such as "a person who uses a wheelchair" or "a person with a hearing impairment." Can you see the difference in these phrases? They put the emphasis on the member as a person rather than seeing his or her identity as the disability or difference.

Elderly

Another special group is the older members of your credit union. Your sensitivity to their individual needs is crucial. Treat elderly members with the same respect you show others. Assume that they are fully capable of handling their own financial affairs unless they ask for help. If an older member indicates that he or she has a disability such as difficulty standing for a long time or a hearing impairment, respond to that disability in the same way you would for any person with a disability.

Some credit unions offer special programs for older members. For example, your credit union might sponsor a Senior Citizens Club, offer senior citizen discounts on community services, or provide special travel services to elderly people. Make sure elderly members are aware of those options so they can take advantage of those special offers.

NEW MEMBERS

New members at your credit union may be young people opening their first financial accounts, new residents to the area, new employees with a company in your credit union's field of membership, or simply consumers attracted by your credit union's mix of products and services.

Especially if they are new to credit unions and/or personal financial management, new members will appreciate the time you take to explain credit union services to them.

- Explain transactions as you complete them. After transferring funds between accounts, for instance, you might say, "Here's the receipt from your share draft account, which shows the withdrawal and your balance there. And here's the receipt showing the deposit in your savings account, along with the new balance."

- Emphasize advantages of credit union membership. Some people who open accounts with credit unions aren't aware they're now members of a financial cooperative. They join the credit union because it offers higher dividend rates than the bank two blocks away, because it's close to home, or because it offers an Internet branch. You can inform them of the other benefits of membership with gentle reminders. For instance, you might say, "Did you notice in our lobby display that we have a special right now on auto loans? As a credit union, we work to keep rates low for everyone."

- Promote other products that might be of value. Many new members may not be familiar with the full range of products and services your credit union offers. For example, a new member may come to your window to check on the balance in her share draft account; she's concerned it may be overdrawn because she forgot to post a check last week. After you help her transfer funds from her share account, you might add, "Ms. Capuano, would you like some information about our overdraft protection plan? It's a line of credit that automatically prevents accidental overdrafts, and it doesn't cost anything until you need it!"

Other Special Situations

Here are two examples of special situations you may encounter as a teller, along with some suggestions about how to deal with them. Your credit union may have established procedures to deal with these and other special member needs.

- If a member is not proficient in English, depend as much as possible on the written numerical information of the transaction to communicate. Use terms the member is familiar with to make sure the transaction is handled to the member's satisfaction. In credit unions that serve specific ethnic areas, one of your coworkers may be bilingual; ask for his or her assistance, or refer the member to that staff member for help with more complex transactions.

- If a member is dealing with an emotional situation, such as a death in the family, be prepared to make special accommodations. Your credit union may have a specific procedure about directing bereaved family members to a private office with a member representative who can help them settle the accounts of their loved ones. Members will appreciate the courtesy of having privacy in such a difficult time. In addition, these transactions may require the special skills of an experienced member representative.

We all have different personalities and preferences. Our families, cultures, education, careers, and interests set us apart—and give us things in common. As you deal regularly with members, you will become more accustomed to picking up cues about how they prefer to interact with you. Every member merits courteous service, but some love to chat, while others prefer a more businesslike interaction. Some members want to go over their transactions in detail with you, while others make it clear they want to complete their dealings as quickly as possible. Recognizing these member preferences will make their experience—and your job—with the credit union more enjoyable and fulfilling.

CHECK IT OUT! ✔

Member Relations

Directions: Each situation below is one that can occur as you work with members. Think about how you would handle each case, then write your response on a separate sheet of paper. Discuss your answers with your supervisor for verification.

1. You ask a member to see some identification. He becomes angry, saying he has been a member at the credit union for fifteen years and shouldn't need to present an ID. What do you do?

2. A moment ago, only two members were at your window. Now, seven are in line and no more backup help is available. What do you do?

3. A little boy, probably three or four years old, has waited quietly with his mother. Now, he goes over to the heavy, padded ropes that cordon off the waiting area and begins swinging on them with such energy that they nearly tip over. His mother ignores him. What do you do?

4. A member using a walker approaches your window. She wants to withdraw $50. She appears to have difficulty supporting herself and opening her billfold at the same time. What do you do?

5. As you prepare to transfer $500 from a share account to a share draft account as the member has requested, you notice the balance of the share account is only $200. What do you do?

6. A long-time member has made it clear on previous visits that she prefers to deal with a specific teller, a neighbor of hers who has served her at the credit union for many years. When you return from lunch, that member is standing at the front of the waiting line, and her regular teller is busy with another member. What do you do?

7. A member whose primary language is Spanish has questions about a fee on his statement. As the line behind him grows, the member responds to your repeated attempts to explain the charge with a confused shake of his head. What do you do?

Your Credit Union Jargon

Directions: Review the terms in figure 3.2. Do you understand the terms and their explanations? Can you think of other terms that confused you when you started working as a teller? If so, list those terms below along with an explanation.

Is there other jargon used in your credit union? If there are terms you occasionally hear but don't understand, write the words or abbreviations below. Ask your supervisor or coworkers what they mean. Then write the word or words to use in place of this jargon when you talk to members.

Jargon   **Translation**

_____

_____

_____

_____

_____

_____

_____

_____

RELATING TO OTHER EMPLOYEES

What do we live for, if it is not to make life less difficult for each other?

—*George Eliot*

In your job as a credit union teller, you have the opportunity to form good relationships with many different groups of people. The people you work with will be of different genders, ages, and cultures; in fact, they will likely be as diverse as the members you serve. That's a plus for the credit union—and it can be positive for you as you discover interesting differences and common interests you share. Members, coworkers, supervisors, and managers all benefit from the interest you demonstrate in them.

Building good relationships with others also benefits *you*. Work is more rewarding when you help someone you care about. Sharing a job with coworkers creates a relaxed, comfortable atmosphere. And, feeling positive about your supervisor and manager strengthens your self-confidence. Maintaining good relationships improves your productivity and makes your job more enjoyable.

RELATING TO YOUR COWORKERS

Although members are your first priority, your coworkers are important, too. You and your fellow employees comprise a team, working together to give your members excellent service and to contribute to your credit union's success. To be a good team member, you depend on other staff as much as on your own abilities. In turn, they depend on you. Therefore, it is in everyone's best interests to establish good relationships with other employees. The following ways to get along with your coworkers are summarized in figure 4.1.

Be Pleasant and Positive

Too obvious? The fact is that most people prefer to work with other people who are pleasant and have a positive outlook. It's more enjoyable to walk into the credit union and exchange a smile and "Good morning" with the other employees. A pleasant manner and upbeat attitude helps you build and maintain good relationships.

A certain amount of socializing on the job helps build productive relationships. Chatting briefly as you start the day or exchanging small talk on a coffee break helps foster good relationships and improves your rapport. However, don't let brief chats turn into extended conversations that interfere with serving members.

Blessed is he who makes his companions laugh.

—The Koran

Appreciate Help

Coworkers often help each other out, and it's important that you show appreciation for that help. Your coworkers may lend a hand in many ways. For example, if you're not sure how to process unusual transactions or how to fill out different

Figure 4.1 Getting Along with Coworkers

- Be pleasant and positive.
- Appreciate help.
- Offer to help.
- Reserve judgment of others.
- Be a joiner.
- Welcome new employees.

forms, a coworker can be a handy and helpful source for this information. You'll also probably feel more comfortable asking questions of coworkers rather than feeling like you're taking up a lot of your supervisor's time. Also, you may have regular tasks, such as filing signature cards, that can be difficult to stay on top of during busy times. If someone frequently answers your questions or offers to help you when you're overloaded, show you appreciate the help.

It's a good idea to let your supervisor know when others have been particularly helpful. A simple statement such as, "I just wanted to let you know Jennifer gave me a hand with that pile of file maintenance yesterday. She just came over and offered to help—I hadn't even asked. I wouldn't have gotten it done without her help." Passing along this kind of appreciation and credit will gain respect from coworkers and your supervisor.

Offer to Help

The flip side of getting help is offering to help others and being willing to help when you're asked. This can be as simple as asking if others need supplies if you're getting some. Or, help someone carry something or hold a door open. At times, you may not realize that a coworker needs help until he or she asks you. If at all possible, try to assist that person willingly. Most coworkers only ask for help when they genuinely need it. Be generous and you'll make the job easier for someone else and be more likely to get help when you need it.

Working for a credit union is a team effort. Even when the lobby is empty of members, you and your fellow tellers can work to maintain a high level of member service. That might mean filing or refilling brochure racks. If you can't come up with a job that needs doing on a slow day, ask a coworker or your supervisor. Staying busy helps the work day pass more pleasantly.

Reserve Judgment of Others

Sometimes you'll find that others are criticizing or exchanging negative stories about coworkers. Try to stay out of this kind of conversation because you seldom get the full story and what you hear is often distorted. This kind of criticism is harmful to others. It contributes to bad feelings and can even ruin careers. If others want you to agree with their negative comments, it's usually best to say you weren't involved and don't have an opinion. You also may be able to point out a different interpretation that is not negative and just as plausible. You'll clearly send a signal that you don't want to get involved in these kinds of conversations.

Be a Joiner

Although you want to stay out of gossip, you also don't want to be too shy or uninvolved. You can show you'd like to have a positive relationship with coworkers in many ways. If the credit union has a picnic or holiday party, try to go and mix with your coworkers in a casual setting. This is the time for those extended conversations.

You may be able to help a coworker who is collecting pledges for a walk-a-thon or other charity activity. Many credit unions get involved in community and charitable activities because they strongly relate to the "people helping people" mission of credit unions. Your involvement in these kinds of activities help you get to know your coworkers and build a good working relationship.

Welcome New Employees

Don't forget how it feels to be the brand-new employee. There is so much to learn that the new employee often feels overwhelmed. You can help by showing support. Welcome your new coworker with a cheerful greeting each day. Make it a point to learn the person's name quickly. Include the employee in lunchtime conversations. Be prepared to explain procedures several times because it's easy to forget parts of the job at first.

RELATING TO YOUR SUPERVISOR

Just as maintaining a good working relationship with coworkers requires effort on your part, so does maintaining a good working relationship with your supervisor. You share the responsibility with your supervisor for the success of your relationship.

Meeting your supervisor's expectations is usually first on an employee's list of objectives. After all, your supervisor is the one who evaluates your performance and has a strong influence on your job future. Trying to meet your supervisor's expectations demonstrates your desire to achieve, your willingness to do the job well, and your awareness that success is a team effort. But sometimes, it's difficult to know how to build a good relationship. Here are six techniques, as listed in figure 4.2, that you can use to strengthen your relationship with your supervisor.

Show Support

For the best success in your job, try to take actions that help make you *and* your supervisor successful. When trying to decide what action to take, ask yourself,

Figure 4.2 Techniques for Working with Your Supervisor

- Show support.
- Learn your supervisor's priorities.
- Admit your mistakes.
- Be open to coaching.
- Register complaints appropriately.
- Recognize supervisors are people, too.

"Will this help make me successful? Will this help make my supervisor successful?" This perspective helps you determine the best ways to support your supervisor. In the long run, it's an important way for you to show respect (after all, he or she is the one in charge) and earn corresponding trust.

Learn Your Supervisor's Priorities

What does your supervisor think is your most important responsibility? What does your supervisor want the staff to improve on? What are the goals that your supervisor is working on? If you can answer these questions accurately, you will make better choices on where to put your best efforts and energy. You may also find that you have certain skills and talents your supervisor values highly. Perhaps your supervisor has to spend quite a bit of time on a project or a big report. You may have skills that relate well to that project and can help out your supervisor. Even the most organized supervisor sometimes thinks that delegating takes more time than it's worth if he or she thinks it involves much additional training. If you already have certain skills, you may be able to help out with only a little training.

Admit Your Mistakes

Do not look where you fell, but where you slipped.

—African proverb

Another way to build trust with your supervisor is to admit when you make a mistake. Most supervisors will respect you if you admit a mistake rather than wait for someone else to tell the supervisor. Even if you correct the problem before you tell the supervisor, it's a good idea to admit it anyway if a member might complain or if you feel the supervisor should know for another reason. In addition, there may be times you have to go to a supervisor and explain a mistake or problem that is not yet resolved. In these situations, your best action is to present your idea of how you might correct the problem or how you will try to prevent it in the future. Your apology and initiative show that you care and want to avoid it happening again.

Be Open to Coaching

The time may come when your supervisor will need to correct or coach your performance. How you handle coaching and criticism tells your supervisor a lot about your character. Be open to what he or she is saying. It's natural to feel defensive if you are being told you did something wrong but try to control that instinct. Listen without interrupting. If you need information clarified, ask matter-of-factly. Decide whether or not you think the supervisor is right. If you agree and understand, assure your supervisor you will work hard not to let it happen again. If you disagree, state what happened calmly. Help your supervisor understand your side, but don't argue. When the discussion is over, work to make the changes in your job performance.

The trouble with most of us is we would rather be ruined by praise than saved by criticism.

—Dr. Norman Vincent Peale

Register Complaints Appropriately

At times, you may feel that you have not been treated fairly or you are not happy about an event or policy. Think before you complain. Ask yourself if the problem will solve itself, if it is important, or if it really interferes with your job. In other words, complain only when you think something must be done or a situation will get worse.

When you do complain, talk to your supervisor privately. State your opinion in a calm, unemotional voice. Give good reasons for your complaint. Offer fair alternatives to the problem.

Then let your supervisor respond. Be open to what he or she has to say. You might be surprised to learn that your supervisor is unaware of the problem or that he or she is aware and is working on a solution. Whether or not the problem is resolved to your complete satisfaction, once your supervisor understands your view and makes a decision, accept it. Use the resolution as an opportunity to continue to build your relationship with your supervisor by respecting his or her decision.

Recognize Supervisors Are People, Too

Supervisors experience job pressures and bad days and, yes, even make mistakes. Just remember that they may need understanding, support, and forgiveness at times. Just as you're not perfect, neither are supervisors. They are fallible people who are trying to do a good job, and sometimes you will need to understand and respect that. They may not deal with as many members as you do on a daily basis but on some days, they may deal with only the angry or unhappy ones. In addition, they are sometimes caught in the middle: it's their job to enforce policies decided by people above them on the organizational ladder with people who report to them. These situations can be particularly challenging and demanding for supervisors.

Remember, even monkeys fall out of trees.

—Korean proverb

Overall, work to develop a good relationship with your supervisor. A supervisor can be a great help in those situations when you are working with a difficult member and need to say, "Would you like to speak to my supervisor?" At those times, if you have developed a good working relationship with your supervisor, you'll be especially glad he or she is there to support you.

Relating to Employees in Other Departments

At the credit union, your relationship with employees in other departments should, above all, focus on cooperation. All employees have duties and responsibilities. Showing your understanding that their work and their jobs are important will help foster the spirit of cooperation and team effort. Many credit unions develop standard procedures to help people in different departments work together as easily and efficiently as possible.

Whenever possible, remember to include coworkers from other departments in your conversations. At after-hour get-togethers, make a point of mixing with everyone, not just other tellers. It's normal to feel most comfortable around those with whom you spend the most time, but make the effort to include others. You'll build relationships with other employees and may even make new friends.

Relating to Senior Management

The management levels above your supervisor are also part of your working relationships. To strengthen your understanding of management responsibilities, read your credit union's policy manual. Become familiar with the organizational chart in your credit union that shows the chain of command. Attend your annual meeting. Ask for additional reading material on the duties of credit union management.

When your president or a board member passes you in the aisle or lobby, take the initiative to greet them and introduce yourself when you first meet them. Don't be intimidated by titles. Your president, officers, and directors—like everyone else—will appreciate your friendliness and recognition.

CHECK IT OUT! ✔

Relating to Coworkers and Employees in Other Departments

Directions: Think about the questions below and put your decisions into action.

1. Has someone in your department been helpful to you in the last week or so? Did they go out of their way to help or respond promptly when you asked? Thank that person and tell them you appreciated it. Let your supervisor know if the other employee was especially helpful.

2. Observe a fellow employee for a week. Observe how he or she interacts with members and coworkers and how he or she talks about work. What positive points can you identify in your coworker's actions and attitudes? What might you learn from your coworker's example?

Relating to Your Supervisor

Directions: For each of the following typical teller responsibilities, circle what you think your supervisor believes is the importance level. List additional responsibilities that are also important. Then, check your answers by talking to your supervisor. Discuss any differences so that you understand and can implement your supervisor's priorities.

| | **Importance** | | |
	Somewhat	Moderately	Very
Processing transactions with a very high degree of accuracy	————	————	————
Showing courtesy to members	————	————	————
Recognizing and greeting board members	————	————	————
Balancing without overages or shortages	————	————	————
Processing transactions as quickly as possible	————	————	————
Promoting services to members	————	————	————
Following policies and procedures "to the letter"	————	————	————
————————————	————	————	————
————————————	————	————	————
————————————	————	————	————

HANDLING CASH AND CHECKS

New Receptionist: "Excuse me, Marge. Is this check OK? It's not a member's—it's actually one of mine."

Teller: "Looks OK to me . . . Oops, wait a minute, that's stale-dated. I'm sorry, but we can't accept it."

New Receptionist: "What do you mean? Stale-dated? How can a check get stale? I thought only bread got stale."

Teller: "Sorry, I should've said it's too old. It's past the time limit for us to accept it. You need to go back to whoever gave it to you and ask for a new one."

New Receptionist: "I was afraid of something like that. It's a birthday present and I was trying to hold off spending it. But Gram called yesterday and told me to cash it because it makes it hard to balance her checkbook. She's gonna love it when I call and tell her it's stale. She'll probably tell me she'll bake me a new one!"

An important technical aspect of your job as a credit union teller is learning and following the correct policies and procedures for handling cash and checks. Although they vary among credit unions, all financial institutions establish rules for these responsibilities. For each of these areas, general guidelines are presented in this chapter to illustrate typical credit union operations. However, be sure to check with your own credit union for its specific rules in these areas. (If you do not handle cash in your job, some of the guidelines in these sections may be useful in your personal life or if you gain cash-handling responsibilities later.)

CASH HANDLING

Each day, from the moment you open your drawer to the time you place your cash tray in the vault, you handle money. And each day represents a new opportunity for you to manage your cash with safety and accuracy. Here are a number of effective cash-handling guidelines that may be part of your credit union's policies and procedures:

1. Always verify cash by counting it at least twice. Three times is better. Whether you're giving or receiving it from a member, or giving or receiving it from the vault, the amount is your responsibility once it passes through your hands. That includes strapped or clipped currency.

2. Limit the amount of cash in your drawer. Return excess amounts to the vault during the day.

3. Always verify identification before handing out cash.

Keep your cash drawer locked at all times when you are away from it.

---

4. Keep your cash drawer locked at all times when you are away from it, even for a moment. Remember you are responsible for every penny and dollar in it.

5. Develop a routine for counting your cash. Decide which way is most comfortable for you to count—by denomination, by unit, or by quantity—and *stick with it!* Begin by counting the largest denomination first and work your way down.

6. Keep your cash drawer neat. Make sure all denominations are separated, and all bills are turned the same way, face up.

7. Do not allow yourself to be interrupted as you count cash. If an interruption is unavoidable, begin your count again.

8. Always hand out coins first, then bills.

9. Develop a routine for the order in which you complete the steps of a transaction.

10. When making change or exchanging currency, leave the original bill on the counter but out of the member's reach until you hand out the change.

11. Use special care when handling new bills. They are likely to stick together.

12. Keep all written calculations and calculator tapes for end-of-day balancing.

13. Count cash by looking at the faces on the bills, not the numbers. (See chapter 6, Security Procedures and Fraud Prevention, for more information on this.)

14. Always verify rolls of coins *before* using them.

15. Check with your supervisor for special procedures when accepting or disbursing large amounts of cash—generally, amounts over $10,000. Government regulations require a Currency Transaction Report be filled out on these transactions. Regulations also require tellers to obtain and record certain information when a member purchases checks or other negotiable instruments in amounts from $3,000 to $10,000.

SHARE DRAFT (CHECK) CASHING

One of the greatest areas of concern for tellers is share draft or check cashing. That's because it requires considerable judgment on the teller's part. Here are some suggestions, summarized in figure 5.1, to assist you with share draft cashing:

1. Find out if your credit union's policy is to cash share drafts only for members.

Figure 5.1 Share Draft Cashing Guidelines

- Know your credit union's share draft cashing policies.
- Make sure the share draft has all necessary and accurate information.
- Verify amounts.
- Have share drafts endorsed in ink in your presence.
- Allow only last endorsee (if more than one) to cash check.
- Verify identification.
- Verify that "on-us" checks are covered.
- Deposit business checks only; do not cash.
- Date stamp all checks.
- Ask your supervisor for help if you are unsure of procedures.

2. Look at the share draft. Make sure it is complete, and not postdated (dated later than today) or stale-dated (dated a set period earlier; typical stale-dating deadlines might be six months to one year).

3. Verify that the amounts on the share draft match. Compare the numbers with the written words.

Verify that the amounts on the share draft match. Compare the numbers with the written words.

---

4. Make sure the share draft is endorsed. Know your credit union's policy on accepting the various types of endorsements that can be used. If you question an endorsement (or it is your credit union's policy), ask the member to sign again in your presence.

5. If more than one person has endorsed the share draft, allow only the last endorser to cash it.

6. Always verify identification, such as a driver's license or other ID acceptable at your credit union, before cashing a share draft.

7. For "on-us" share drafts (share drafts drawn on the credit union), determine if enough money is in the account to cover the share draft, or if a stop payment or hold order has been placed on the account.

8. For share drafts made out to businesses, only deposit them; do not cash them. If an authorized user desires cash, he or she can make a withdrawal of the same amount after the draft is deposited.

9. Stamp or initial all share drafts you accept, according to your credit union's policies.

10. Ask your supervisor (in private) for help whenever you are unsure about cashing a share draft.

SHARE DRAFT (CHECK) HOLDS

Another area that requires a teller's professional attention is share draft or check holds. Although a share draft drawn on another institution represents money, there is no way to be certain that enough money exists to cover it until the share draft clears. Sometimes, even when the share draft appears satisfactory and the payee is a member, it's best to place a condition on the share draft's acceptance. This condition is called a **hold.** Know your credit union's share draft hold policies and procedures.

When you place a hold on a member's account, you temporarily restrain the member's use of an amount of money in that account. During that period, the share draft or check you accepted should have time to clear. But how does a teller decide which share drafts justify placing a hold on a member's funds? And how long is the hold? This is one area of credit union policy that is determined by both good business practices and government regulation.

Under the Expedited Funds Availability Act (implemented through Regulation CC), financial institutions have specific limits on which checks they can place holds and how long those holds can be. This means that although your credit union can have hold policies that are less restrictive than the law requires, it cannot have policies that are more restrictive. For example, if a financial institution cannot put a hold longer than five days on a certain type of check, your credit union could establish a policy that would put a shorter hold on that check. However, it couldn't establish a standard hold of longer than five days.

Why are rules like these important to you? If you know that certain holds have regulatory restrictions on how they are applied, you have a better understanding when supervisors make exceptions or say they can't make exceptions because of check hold laws.

You will need to know your credit union's policies, but here are some general guidelines on when to place share draft or check holds. These guidelines define the types of checks, but not the minimum holds. Check your credit union's policies for that information.

- Share drafts or checks presented by new members with accounts less than 30 days old
- Large deposits, totaling $5,000 or more
- Share drafts or checks for deposit into an account that has had repeated overdrafts
- Large personal share drafts or checks
- Business share drafts or checks from a company you do not recognize
- Out-of-town share drafts or checks

Remember: No rule requires that that you must accept a share draft or check simply because a member hands it to you. You have the option to place a hold according to your credit union's policy or refuse the share draft. For new tellers, the best idea is to ask your supervisor before placing a hold. With experience, you'll become more confident in knowing whether or not holds are needed.

TIPS FOR ACCURATE CASH AND CHECK HANDLING

Another skill you need is the *ability to work accurately with numbers*. While accuracy on the job is always important, it is even more so at a credit union. The numbers you deal with represent members' money, and members have placed their trust in your ability to handle their accounts correctly. Following are tips that will help you increase your accuracy in handling cash and checks. See figure 5.2 for a summary of these tips.

Get in the habit of *rechecking your numbers*. Part of being accurate is realizing that no one is correct on the first try one hundred percent of the time. Double-check account numbers and amounts written on transaction tickets. Recheck your calculations and retain the calculator tapes. Also, habitually triple-counting money before disbursing it is an obvious sign of an accurate teller. When counting out cash to a member, these are the three counts that can prevent giving out the wrong amount:

First: Count the cash as you take it from your cash drawer.
Second: Count the cash to yourself as you count it out on the counter or hand-to-hand.
Third: Count the cash aloud as you count it out to the member.

Be organized in your work area. Keep your counter area neat and put away cash and documents immediately after use. In this way, you will avoid misplacing or losing important documents. You will also know that all business with one member has been finished before you start on a transaction for another member.

Establish and follow *systems and standard procedures* in your work. This doesn't mean simply following your credit union's established procedures. This also means conducting transactions according to a standard routine so that certain steps are followed

Figure 5.2 Tips for Accurately Handling Cash and Checks

- Recheck your numbers.
- Be organized in your work area.
- Follow your own systems and standard procedures.
- Concentrate on one transaction at a time.
- Work at a quick but steady pace when busy.

almost automatically. For example, for transactions where you are giving cash to a member, some tellers always give the cash as the last step in the procedure. Why? An important reason is that then they won't accidentally give the cash twice (yes, this does happen!). Also, since most members will not leave before they receive the cash, it is a way to ensure that all details have been taken care of before the member walks away. An alternative approach is to complete all transactions before responding to members' questions or request for information.

Concentrate on and *finish one transaction or activity before you move on* to the next. The temptation to do two things at once is especially strong if you are handling two drive-through lanes or working a teller window and also managing a drive-through lane. Your accuracy may suffer if you are switching back and forth between two transactions. Be especially careful if this happens or finish one transaction before starting another.

Another way to make sure you concentrate on one activity at a time is to watch for and control interruptions in your work. Interruptions do occur but if you are in the middle of a calculation, counting cash, or other number-intensive activities, it's a good idea to start over.

Errors can occur if you are trying to work too quickly on a busy day.

Sometimes in the pressure of a busy day, you may think you can finish filling out certain forms or process certain credits or debits later. This is typically not a good idea. Certainly, your credit union may allow some delay in handling certain routine file maintenance activities such as processing a change of address. But building up too many bits and pieces of unfinished or unprocessed work can reduce your overall accuracy.

Finally, one area that can cause errors is trying to work too quickly on a busy day. Certainly, the ability to work quickly with numbers is a skill you must have. But it must complement your commitment to be accurate. Some people have a talent for working quickly, but make mistakes as they go. Others are cautiously correct, but unable to work fast. Try to *work at a steady rate* that achieves quick work without sacrificing accuracy. In the long run, this saves more time because it prevents errors and work that must be corrected.

If you follow these tips, you will increase your accuracy while maintaining quality member service.

WHEN MISTAKES HAPPEN

Money is a sensitive issue for all of us, so any mistake—no matter how small—has the potential to shake a member's confidence in the credit union. Accuracy is essential. Credit union tellers make mistakes on only a small percent of the work they do for members. But because tellers handle so many transactions, even that small percentage means you'll see errors once in a while.

The way you handle the mistakes members bring to your attention can help restore their confidence in the credit union. The same is true of mistakes you discover before members notice them. Regardless of how a problem comes to light, you have two issues to address: correcting the mistake and satisfying the member.

Figure 5.3 lists some of the types of errors you'll see most often. Fortunately, most errors are easy to fix. Your credit union will train you on who should make the corrections and how to handle them.

Even a mistake may turn out to be the one thing necessary to a worthy achievement.

—Henry Ford

Satisfying the member is often more complex. When a member says the credit union made a mistake, listen carefully. You need to identify the immediate problem so it can be fixed. But the original error may have caused the member additional fees, embarrassment, or other problems. One example is a share draft being returned for insufficient funds because a deposit was erroneously placed in a member's share savings account instead of the share draft account. You must address those other issues as well. If the member is irate, use suggestions offered in chapter 3.

- Offer a simple apology. Sometimes all a member needs is an acknowledgment that he or she is right. Try not to get defensive, even if it was your mistake. The reasons for an error may matter to you, but they usually sound like excuses to a member. Sometimes a member causes an error or contributes to it in some way. But think carefully before saying anything that implies the member is at fault. You'll probably only create bad feelings when you want to make the member feel good about doing business with the credit union.

Figure 5.3 Common Errors Affecting Credit Union Members

Here are the types of mistakes you'll probably have to help members with most often. Note that many of them are errors made by tellers—and most of them are easy to prevent.

Incorrect transactions

- Teller selected the wrong type of account, such as share draft instead of share savings.
- Teller selected wrong member's account.
- Teller entered the wrong transaction code (such as withdrawal instead of deposit).
- Teller entered cash or checks incorrectly.
- Teller missed a transaction, or part of one (such as forgetting to distribute cash back).

Cash given incorrectly

- Teller gave cash twice.
- Teller didn't give any cash back.
- Teller gave wrong amount.

Share drafts ordered incorrectly

- Employee typed information wrong.
- Employee didn't make changes the member requested.
- Teller didn't verify information for share draft order.

Automated transactions incorrect

- Employees set up transactions wrong.
- Employees failed to set up transactions at all.
- Employees didn't make changes or didn't make them correctly.
- Employees didn't communicate necessary information to the member.

What can you do to avoid most of these errors? Make a point of reading transaction slips carefully. Look at everything written on the slip. Ask about anything that isn't perfectly clear. Check to be sure the information on your computer screen matches the transaction slip (name, totals, account numbers, amount of cash back, etc.). Always double-check. In fact, triple-checking never hurts!

- Take ownership of the issues. You may need to research something and communicate the results to the member later. Follow up as needed, and do it in a timely fashion. If you can't take care of everything yourself, check up on things later to be sure everything got resolved.

- Go the limit your credit union allows to satisfy the member. Some credit unions may refund their own fees or pay extra costs a member incurs as a result of a credit union error. Some will write letters on the member's behalf to explain something that was not a member's fault. Some may send flowers, gift certificates, or other appropriate items as an apology for the member's inconvenience. Ask your supervisor about your credit union's guidelines in this area.

- Think about what you can do to prevent the error from happening again. Will sharing information about a process help your member avoid the same type of problem in the future? Did some credit union system or procedure contribute to the mistake? Do you need to change the way you do something? Anything you can do to help eliminate errors is a valuable service to members—and to the credit union!

Be an entrepreneur of your dept.
Suggest better processes
Who has an emp. suggestion program?

CHECK IT OUT! ✔

Cash Handling Techniques

Directions: Review the cash-handling techniques in this chapter and select three that you think are particularly important in your credit union. List them below. Discuss these points with your supervisor.

1.

2.

3.

Draft (Check) Handling Techniques

Directions: Answer the following questions and check your answers with your supervisor.

1. What is your credit union's policy on stale-dated checks? Postdated checks?

2. What is acceptable identification at your credit union? List examples below.

3. What are your credit union's hold policies for local checks/drafts?

4. What are your credit union's hold policies for non-local checks?

5. What are other hold policies you must know?

Resolving Problems

Ask your supervisor about credit union policies for compensating members for fees paid because of a credit union mistake. List those policies below.

_____

_____

_____

_____

_____

_____

_____

_____

_____

_____

_____

_____

_____

_____

_____

_____

_____

_____

SECURITY PROCEDURES AND FRAUD PREVENTION

The numbers help tell the story about fraud against U.S. credit unions:

- *In 1998, credit unions filed 9,000 check fraud claims, totaling $22 million (compared to 5,500 claims totaling $10 million in 1995).*[1]

- *Check fraud takes several forms, the most common of which are forgery (34%), counterfeiting and alteration (27%), writing checks on closed accounts (17%), and kiting (10%).*[2]

- *Just over half of all credit unions report check fraud losses each year.*[3]

Fraud and other financial crimes have an increasingly damaging impact on credit unions—and their members. Your members trust you to protect their accounts. If lapses in security and fraud occur, your credit union must not only replace the lost money (which will reduce dividends returned to members), but it may also be liable for fines and other legal costs. As the headlines included throughout this chapter report, financial crimes can levy a heavy toll on credit unions. As a teller, you can help prevent losses.

---

1. From "Steps to Cut Check-Fraud Losses," p. 1, *Credit Union Executive Newsletter*, April 19, 1999.

2. From "Fighting Fraud Today," p. 7, *Credit Union Journal*, June 24, 1998.

3. From "Share Draft Growth Adding to Fraud Problems," p. 1, *Credit Union News*, January 24, 1997.

"The (Funny) Money Supply is Soaring"

—Business Week

Your job success depends on careful and honest work. One of your top responsibilities is keeping an eye out for possible fraud. To handle fraud situations, you will receive additional training from your credit union. To begin, here is an overview of the types of information you'll need to know. (See figure 6.1 for a summary.)

INTERNAL CONTROLS

Internal controls are required actions that help protect cash and other assets and maintain accurate financial records. Examples of internal controls are approval limits on cash withdrawals, check number records, teller stamps, computer passwords, and limitations on which employees have access to the vault and other secured areas or records. All credit unions have internal controls because part of protecting members' assets is avoiding any action that even *appears* inappropriate. Following are typical internal controls that will affect your job.

Personal Transactions

Just like employees in other businesses who "shop" where they work, you are likely to have accounts at your credit union. Know your credit union's policy on how to handle your personal credit union business. Some credit unions require employee transactions

Figure 6.1 Internal Controls for Tellers

- Avoid any action that may appear inappropriate.
- Never handle your own or a family member's account.
- Treat coworker transactions as if they were member transactions, without special favors.
- Never use a kitty to help balance your drawer.
- Avoid sharing drawers with others.
- Lock your drawer whenever you are away from it.

to be handled by the supervisor. If this is not required, you should follow normal procedures, as if you were any member transacting credit union business. Go to another teller in front of, not behind, the counter or drive-through, and follow all the standard rules. When other employees come to your window, handle their transactions as you would handle member transactions. Treat their business with the same internal controls and confidentiality. And treat them equally courteously because you know they won't hesitate to say they'll take their business elsewhere!

Small Overages and Shortages

Many tellers are proud of their accurate balancing record. They seldom need to report even a few cents "over" or "short." However, this can happen occasionally. Large differences are researched and resolved (usually a paper error is found). Small differences are usually noted and may not be resolved. If you have a small difference, never use a "kitty" to help you balance your drawer. It may seem that making up a few cents difference in your cash drawer from your own pocket is a minor point, but doing so inevitably causes problems and is unacceptable.

Cash Drawer Access

You are responsible for the cash in your own drawer. To maintain good control, make sure you do not share a drawer with anyone. If you allow someone else access to it, you are inviting possible problems.

Finally, be sure to lock your drawer whenever you are away from it—no matter what time of day or how long you will be gone. As one internal auditor used to say, "Don't tempt another employee into dishonesty." Depending on the design of your teller counters, it may also be possible for a member to reach across and open your drawer when you are away from it.

Fraud Prevention

"Bank Fraud Crackdown in Chicago"

—American Banker

Many schemes are used to swindle money from financial institutions. As a teller, you are often the first line of defense against certain types of fraud.

The first point you should learn about possible fraud is that it *does* happen and you need to be sensitive for any clues that make you uneasy about a transaction or person at your window. It's always safer to go to a supervisor and have him or her tell you "it's OK" than to let something odd go unexamined and regret it later. You need to develop a balance between maintaining a healthy awareness and looking for fraud in every transaction. After all, the overwhelming majority of your members are honest; even if they give you counterfeit currency or a forged check, they may have received it innocently. Experience and further training will help you achieve an appropriate balance between paranoia and gullibility. In the meantime, here are examples of fraudulent schemes so that you can start developing your sensitivity to the types of situations that may occur.

Forgeries and Altered Share Drafts or Checks

A **forgery** usually involves a genuine share draft or check on which a criminal either signs a fraudulent signature or alters information (such as the amount) on the draft or check. The criminal steals someone else's share drafts and fakes an ID to cash them, or alters the share drafts to a different payee name and then pretends to be the new payee.

"Check Fraud Battle Reaches New Level"

—Bank Systems & Technology

Another form of fraud is altering share draft amounts. For example, a seven dollar share draft may be changed to seventy by adding "ty" to the word "seven" in the written amount, and a 0 after the number 7 in the numerical amount. In these cases, the crook may try to escape detection by depositing part of the share draft amount and asking for the rest in cash. Less suspicion is raised that way than if the entire share draft were cashed. This fraud is often successful when the criminal puts pressure on a teller, such as complaining about the wait or hinting that one of the credit union officers is a personal friend.

Counterfeit Cash and Checks

Another source of fraud is counterfeit cash and checks. Counterfeit cash used to be more difficult to make because the complex and detailed designs on U.S. currency were difficult and expensive to reproduce using available printing technology. However, counterfeiters can now use high-quality color photocopiers and computers with laser printers. Today, this equipment is fairly inexpensive and produces high-quality images.

Due to these threats, the U.S. government continues to introduce new design elements that are more effective against counterfeiting. Paper currency printed since 1990 features microprinting (words that can be read under a magnifying glass but blur when copied or scanned) and security threads of polymer strips visible under bright light and designed to glow a distinctive color for each denomination under ultraviolet light.

The U.S. Treasury is currently redesigning all paper currency; thus far, the new $50, $100, and $20 notes in Series 1996 have been released. The new $10 and $5 notes are the next bills scheduled for release, and the final new design will be for $1 bills. Additional security features of Series 1996 bills include:

- larger, off-center portraits;
- reproduction of the portrait as a watermark (an image impressed in the paper during manufacture that only shows when held to the light);
- color-shifting ink in the number on the lower right corner of the bill fronts that changes from green to black when viewed from different angles;
- fine-line printing patterns in the background of the portrait and on the back of the notes that do not copy or scan well.

The new $20 note also has a machine-readable capability that has been incorporated for the blind, but scanning devices that will be developed to identify the note may also be used to identify bills as authentic.

Stay alert to these changes in bill design to make sure you know what to look for if you suspect counterfeit cash.

"Cards Aren't Only Area of Fraud"

—Credit Union Executive

Altered (or raised) currency can also cause losses to a credit union. Altered currency is produced by cutting one end off of each of two larger denomination bills (such as tens or twenties) and taping or pasting them to the ends of a one dollar bill. The altered one dollar bill is passed off as the larger denomination bill while the larger denomination "mutilated" bills can be redeemed for full value because they meet the minimum requirements for redemption. Counting the portraits on the bills instead of just the ends will more likely uncover this type of deception. With their new designs, the Series 1996 notes are intended to stop the creation of raised currency.

Counterfeit checks are also often produced by copying genuine checks with color photocopiers or creating them in computer software. These checks are a significant threat because their appearance is very close to genuine checks. However, check printing companies are fighting back against this type of crime. Just as currency is starting to include new features, newer checks are also including special features to foil copying and counterfeiting. These include watermarks in the paper, microprinting, special papers, special inks, and nonreproducible designs. As these features vary on different checks, some check printers are specifically listing the special features on the backs of checks. Look for these special features and learn which ones are used on your credit union share drafts.

Some financial software packages for use at home and by small businesses may permit users to print checks on their laser and ink jet printers. Find out if your credit union has a policy about accepting these checks.

In addition to learning about and using these special measures to protect your credit union, share this information with your members. They may even ask you about fraud prevention as they notice the special measures you and your coworkers are taking. Help your members protect themselves from becoming victims of fraud by educating them.

Check Kiting

Another form of fraud is called **check kiting.** The member uses accounts at two or more institutions to take advantage of the float to run a scam. **Float** is the period between the time a check is deposited at a financial institution and the time the institution actually gets money back through the Federal Reserve.

Here's how it works: A kiter deposits a check at your credit union. That check is from his or her account at another financial institution, but there isn't money at that other institution to cover the check. Before it can bounce, the kiter deposits a share draft from your credit union into the other account. When the first check arrives, the kiter appears to have enough money to cover it. This process can continue for some time as the kiter writes larger and larger checks against the accounts to keep the scam going.

Many members make perfectly legitimate deposits drawn on their accounts at other financial institutions. Kiters tend to show a pattern of more frequent deposits (sometimes as often as every day or every few days), followed by withdrawals of nearly equal amounts soon afterward. If you notice suspicious activity of this type, talk to your supervisor. The credit union can use check holds to disrupt what may be a kiting scheme.

As you can see, fraud can occur in many ways. No common description exists for criminals and scam artists. Stay alert at all times as you handle transactions. Examine all share drafts carefully. Keep your eyes on your cash. *Never bend the rules your credit union has established.* Figure 6.2 lists additional safeguards. These are the best ways you can avoid being an innocent accomplice to fraud. You will learn others in your career.

Embezzlement

The form of fraud in which an employee is not an innocent participant is called **embezzlement,** which refers to an employee taking credit union money for personal use. No matter how you try to phrase it, embezzlement is stealing. Whether a few dollars for lunch or a few dimes for a candy bar are taken from the cash drawer during the day, or a complicated plan is used to swindle thousands, the intention is the same.

Many credit unions are now asking all employees to sign a fraud policy similar to that shown in figure 6.3.

Figure 6.2 Additional Safeguards Against Fraud

- Scrutinize the forms of ID closely as you cash a share draft.
- Examine the check to be cashed. Look for damage to account number codes. Check the spelling of the name on the endorsement (you'd be surprised how often criminals misspell an account holder's name).
- When opening new accounts, verify the home address, place of employment, and field of membership. New-account fraud is a growing problem.
- Learn and use your credit union's procedures on employing holds to prevent fraud.
- Do not damage forged checks or other evidence of fraud.

Figure 6.3 Sample Employee Fraud Policy

ABC Federal Credit Union considers any form of fraud or dishonesty on the part of its employees as totally unacceptable conduct. Acts that are considered to be either fraudulent or dishonest include, but are not limited to, the following:

1. Manipulation of loan accounts, documents, computer records, shares, or share draft accounts.

2. Theft of any kind, including stealing from members' accounts, overpayment of dividends, or creating fictitious loans.

3. Check/share draft kiting.

4. Forgeries.

5. Unauthorized or unapproved salary advances or overtime reimbursement.

6. Intentional violation of credit union rules, internal controls, regulations, or procedures.

7. Intentional failure to secure collateral to properly record a security interest in collateral, or to pledge a member's shares as collateral without that member's permission.

8. Granting or requesting preferential treatment for *anyone*.

I have read the above fraud policy. I understand that management will not tolerate fraudulent or dishonest activities of any kind and that I am not to engage in acts of fraud or dishonesty while employed at ABC Federal Credit Union.

_____   _____
Your Signature   Supervisor's Signature

_____   _____
Date   Date

CHECK IT OUT! ✔

Learn about Anti-Fraud Measures

Directions: Find out the information below to become more knowledgeable about anti-fraud measures.

1. Ask your supervisor or another teller to show you the anti-counterfeiting measures currently used in U.S. currency. These change as new technology is introduced so you'll need to make sure you stay up-to-date.

2. Ask your supervisor or a coworker if anti-counterfeiting measures are currently used on your credit union's share drafts. If they are, learn about them in detail.

3. Find out how your credit union ensures the security of its Internet branch and automated phone service. Although these services do not affect your job directly, members often have questions about how safe electronic services are.

Responding to Possible Fraud

Directions: Review the situations below and write down on a separate piece of paper how you would respond. Discuss your answers with your supervisor.

1. A person comes to your window with a check that has already been endorsed and argues with you about re-signing it. When he finally does, the signature doesn't look quite the same. What do you do?

2. A member you know gives you a check that doesn't look quite right. The written amount seems rather cramped-looking and the handwriting on the whole check doesn't seem consistent. The member tells you she received the check as payment for money someone borrowed from her. What do you do?

3. Someone hands you a stack of currency to count before exchanging for smaller bills. What do you do to make sure the currency is genuine?

4. A member gives you a local check dated three days from now and asks you to deposit it. They assure you the check will clear but they just forgot to write the correct date. What do you do?

5. You start to process a deposit and realize that one of the checks isn't actually a check—it's a credit memo from a catalog company. What do you do?

RESPONDING TO EMERGENCIES

DATELINE: *Chatsworth, California*

"I was thunderstruck when I realized the epicenter of an earthquake that registered 6.7 on the Richter scale had occurred just a half mile from my credit union's headquarters . . . Aftershocks continued all morning . . . Most employees struggled through the day, knowing the members were depending on us."

$\mathbf{A}$ teller's job is anything but routine. However, sometimes situations occur that are quite extraordinary compared to what you normally encounter. Such emergencies may never happen in your credit union, but it's best to be prepared just in case. The credit union staff in the news story above were prepared and reacted well in their situations.

Remember the fire drills you had in school? Their purpose was to establish a plan and to train everyone involved in how to carry it out. That way, if a fire occurred, everyone took the correct action with little confusion or questioning. The same type of preparation will help you take the right actions if an emergency occurs at your credit union.

At your credit union, you should have plans for handling the following emergencies:

- Robbery
- Serious member illness
- Power failure and system shutdown
- Fire

- Natural disasters
- Bomb threat
- Kidnapping

In this chapter, you'll review basic tips for responding to these types of emergencies. You'll also receive initial and refresher training at your credit union to keep you up-to-date on the correct procedures that are special to your credit union. Make sure you always know what to do in case of any emergency.

ROBBERY

Concern about robbery is natural for tellers. Although rare, it can happen to any credit union and any teller. Make sure you understand how to respond appropriately and without hesitation. Listed below are basic steps you should take if a robbery occurs at your window.

1. Stay calm. Concentrate on remembering the actions to take.
2. Follow the robber's instructions exactly.
3. Activate your alarm/camera during the robbery, but *only* if you can do so without the robber realizing it. If you have any doubts, activate the alarm after the robber leaves the window.
4. Give the robber your bait money or dye pack from your cash drawer.
5. Keep the note if the robber uses one. Just slide it to the side. If the robber specifically asks for it back, return it.
6. Remember the physical description of the robber (see figure 7.1). Your credit union will have a standard description form. Study it in advance.
7. After the robber leaves your window, watch as he or she leaves the office and note the direction he or she takes. Lock your cash drawer and notify your supervisor. He or she will make sure the police or other authorities are immediately notified. Your supervisor or another employee will also secure the area by blocking off your window and locking the doors.
8. Fill out a description form immediately. Only discuss the robbery with credit union officials and police.
9. Refer questions from the press to your supervisor.

Figure 7.1 Typical Items on a Robber Description Form

- Height
- Weight
- Sex
- Age
- Build
- Hair (color and style)
- Beard/facial hair
- Eyes (color and appearance)
- Glasses (if any)
- Complexion

- Nose (description)
- Teeth (description)
- Shape of face, chin, eyebrows, etc.
- Scars, marks, and other characteristics
- Clothing (type and description)
- Jewelry
- Weapon
- Speech (description of voice, words, etc.)
- Method of escape (vehicle, if any noted)

The most important point you should remember is *safety first*. The safety of employees and members is your highest priority. Toward that end, do not attempt to keep the robber from leaving. Everyone is safer once the robber has left the building and the doors are locked behind him or her.

Finally, about once a month or so, briefly review the list above and think about your credit union's other robbery guidelines. Find out what you should do if a fellow teller is robbed. Robberies are rare, but if you are prepared, you will take the right actions.

SERIOUS MEMBER ILLNESS

A member faints in the lobby. Or perhaps someone complains of chest pains. If you see a member in distress, immediate steps should be taken to attend to the member:

1. Quickly lock your cash drawer.
2. Stay with the member and ask another employee to call an ambulance or vice versa. Also, alert a supervisor.
3. Ask other members to stand back.
4. Make the member comfortable.

5. Find out if any family member or friend has accompanied the member. If not, have another employee notify a relative or other appropriate person.

6. When the ambulance arrives, stand back and let the paramedics work. Be ready to answer questions.

7. Refer all inquiries from the press to your supervisor.

Keep in mind that when the unexpected happens in front of many people, the tendency is not to react. It's easy to assume someone else will take charge. Don't wait for the other person to act. If a member becomes ill, react immediately.

FIRE

DATELINE: Los Angeles
"A fire in the roof above the computer room didn't do much damage . . . but the water that put it out devastated the equipment."

In a matter of minutes, a small fire can change into a roaring blaze. If fire is detected at your credit union, don't waste time. If your immediate safety is not in jeopardy, take these steps:

1. Lock your cash drawer.
2. Immediately call the fire department.
3. Evacuate the members and staff.
4. If possible, during the evacuation, take cash and valuables to the vault and lock it.
5. Leave the building.
6 Lock the door if your credit union's procedures require it.
7. Establish a place where all employees are to meet outside the building to make sure everyone is safe.
8 If you share a building with other businesses, notify them.
9. Refer any inquiries from the press to your supervisor.

Obviously, it will take more than one person to accomplish all these steps. Decide ahead of time each employee's responsibility if a fire breaks out. For example, certain employees could be responsible for helping evacuate members in the lobby. Other employees could be responsible for making sure staff and members in other areas are alerted and evacuated.

Know your credit union's policies and procedures in case of fire. For example, your credit union may have a designated fire team who receives special training.

POWER FAILURE AND SYSTEM SHUTDOWN

A thunderstorm is raging and you're in the middle of a transaction, when suddenly all power goes off. The building is dark and your computer does not work. Seconds go by and power is not restored. In this situation, you should:

1. Lock your cash drawer.
2. Lock the credit union door.
3. If you can't complete the transaction, make a written note of where you were in the process when the power failed.
4. Ask the member and any others in line if they would prefer to wait in the lobby or come back later.
5. Make sure someone contacts the power company.
6. Refer all inquiries from the press to your supervisor.

The amount of time for which power is out will determine additional steps you need to take. Your supervisor or a credit union officer can tell you what should be done.

A more common problem than power outages for many credit unions is computer system shutdowns. Find out what your credit union's policy is for processing transactions during a system outage. For example, some credit unions place restrictions on the amount of cash back during deposit transactions when the computer system is down and you cannot check account balances. Deposit receipts printed during a system shutdown will not show account balances. (System capabilities vary widely. Some computer systems will continue to print receipts but will not show current balances. Others may not operate at all, in which case hand-written receipts may be necessary.) Does your credit union policy direct you to mail receipts showing balances to members who request them once the system is back up?

NATURAL DISASTERS

DATELINE: West Des Moines
". . . the first floor was under three feet of water for two
days after the nearby Raccoon River, a tributary of the
Mississippi River, flooded. Advance flood warnings
helped minimize the damage. We moved computer
equipment and everything else we could to the second
floor as the water was rising."

Hurricanes, tornadoes, earthquakes, and floods can all cause devastating damage, often with no warning at all. If you work in an area where these occur, remember that the safety of members and employees must be protected immediately.

1. Know your credit union's disaster plan ahead of time.
2. Know ahead of time where members and employees should take shelter, and get them there quickly.
3. Lock your cash drawer, or if possible, take cash and valuables to the vault.
4. Concentrate on maintaining your professional behavior and think *safety first.*
5. Return to your station only when it is safe to do so. If the credit union must close for the remainder of the day, ask your supervisor if and how you should report the daily work you have completed so far.
6. Know your credit union's policies and procedures, and follow them.
7. Refer all inquiries from the press to your supervisor.

BOMB THREATS

Today, bomb threats are more frequent than in the past. But the likelihood is still rare that you will receive a phone call from someone who says a bomb has been planted at the credit union. Nevertheless, you should know what to do in such a situation.

1. Try to transfer the call to your president or manager. If you can do this, call the police immediately. If the caller refuses, follow the steps below.

---

2. Use a predetermined signal to tell a nearby employee what is happening, but do so without letting the caller know. The employee should inform your supervisor and call the police.

3. Ask for information. Ask where the bomb is located, what kind of bomb it is, and when it will go off. Take notes. Try to write down everything the caller says.

4. Ask what the caller wants. If you receive instructions, write them and repeat them back.

5. Tell the caller you will meet the demands, and ask for time to do so.

6. Listen carefully. Pay attention to the caller's voice for any clues it can give you about the person speaking. Also listen for background noises that might provide information about the caller's location.

7. After the call, notify police and answer all questions they have.

8. If the building is evacuated, lock all valuables in the vault.

9. Refer all inquiries from the press to your supervisor.

10. Know your credit union's policies and procedures, and follow them.

DATELINE: New York
"The bomb took out three floors and knocked out all power, the emergency generator, and the sprinkler system. The credit union's thirteen-member staff, plus seven board members who were there at the time for a committee meeting, descended fourteen flights of a smoke-filled stairway in total darkness."

Instead of a bomb threat, your credit union could experience a bomb being detonated in the vicinity of the credit union. Or, a major accident such as a gas or chemical explosion could occur nearby. In these instances, many of the guidelines for natural disasters may apply.

KIDNAPPING

Another rare occurrence is the kidnapping of a credit union employee or family member. If you receive a call from someone claiming to have taken a hostage, the steps you should use are similar to those for a bomb threat:

1. Try to transfer the call to someone with more authority. If you can't, follow the steps below.

2. Signal a nearby coworker to inform your supervisor, but do so without letting the caller know.

3. Listen for clues.

4. Take notes.

5. Ask to speak to the hostage. If you can't, ask for proof with questions that will verify if the hostage is with the caller. Your human resources department should maintain personal data sheets on each employee. This may help if verification is needed.

6. Ask what the caller wants. Write down the instructions and repeat them.

7. Ask for other information. Stay on the phone as long as possible.

8. Tell the caller you will meet the demands, and ask for time to do so.

9. After the call, notify police. Answer all their questions.

10. If asked to do so, help with a telephone search for the person identified as a hostage. Call home, work, or any place the person may be. Call neighbors, friends, and relatives to find out if they know where the person is.

11. Refer all inquiries from the press to your supervisor.

Often the caller will be attempting to extort money without actually having kidnapped anyone. If so, the caller will make sure ahead of time that the "hostage" can't be reached by phone. And you will be given a short amount of time to meet the demand. The longer you have, the more likely you'll be able to contact the "hostage." That's why all credit union employees need to keep a current list of contacts on file. This list should be used as quickly as possible after the threat is made. Always notify the credit union immediately of any changes in address, phone number, vehicle, or relatives to notify in case of emergency.

Remember, in an emergency, the most important steps you can take are to stay calm, use your head, and remain professional. To be able to accomplish these steps effectively, review the procedures periodically and make sure you'll know what to do. If an emergency does happen, your practice and training will pay off.

CHECK IT OUT! ✔

Emergency Situations

Directions: Check your credit union's procedures and talk to your supervisor about emergency situations. Then write the first three steps you would take in the situations listed below.

During Robbery

1.

2.

3.

After Robbery

1.

2.

3.

Fire

1.

2.

3.

Member who faints or is otherwise ill

1.

2.

3.

Power failure

1.

2.

3.

Computer system shutdown

1.

2.

3.

Bomb threat

1.

2.

3.

Natural disaster or nearby accident

1.

2.

3.

Kidnapping

1.

2.

3.

Your Signature

Date

Supervisor's Signature

Date

TAKING RESPONSIBILITY FOR YOUR JOB SUCCESS

If people only knew how hard I work to gain my mastery, it wouldn't seem so wonderful at all.

—*Michelangelo*

In this chapter, we include words of advice from a diverse group of highly successful people on taking personal responsibility for your future. In particular, this chapter can give you ideas on implementing your plans for success as a credit union teller.

DEVELOPING YOUR TELLER QUALITIES

A teller's job involves both technical and communication skills that you learn through training and experience. But these are not the only elements you need to be a successful teller. You also have personal characteristics that qualified you for the job in the first place and that you can further develop.

People Orientation

Above all, credit union tellers are "people persons." They like people. Seeing new faces every day, helping someone with a problem, and having enjoyable conversations with others all make the job rewarding and fun.

If that seems pretty obvious, consider that not all employees are people-oriented. Some would much rather work with documents and objects. Some may be shy around people, prefer an independent work environment, or have a knack for mechanical things. In any case, dealing with people takes more effort for them.

People orientation involves liking people, caring about their interests and problems, and showing empathy and understanding. It means helping others and remaining patient in your interactions with members and coworkers. These qualities have value and importance in your job success so don't take them for granted! Recognize that they're special qualities not everyone has. They are the skills that will make you especially successful as a credit union teller.

Control Under Pressure

Keep your face to the sunshine and you cannot see the shadow.

—Helen Keller

Likewise, the ability to maintain your self-control under pressure is important. Not everyone can. Some people make a lot of mistakes when pressured. Others become irritable. That doesn't mean they're not hard-working. It simply indicates they need a different work environment. Good tellers work well even when pressure creates stress. Long lines and irate members come with the job. When you face these situations pleasantly, politely, and even with a sense of humor, you show you can control yourself and the situation.

Honesty and Ethics

Honesty is important to any employer, but it is particularly significant to a credit union. Handling members' financial accounts requires absolute honesty. Your job is to safeguard member's funds and avoid misuse of funds or other property.

Ethical behavior is also a quality that underlies a teller's success. Some parts of the job have standards that go beyond simple honesty. For example, ethical employees do not take advantage of their positions for personal gain. Your good judgment tells you whether you could be taking advantage of your position. For example, accepting home-made holiday cookies from a member would be perfectly all right. So would keeping a complimentary ballpoint pen from an insurance representative. However, accepting any gift of greater than token value, particularly if it is exchanged for the way an account is handled, is not acceptable. Your credit union will have additional rules that deal with this area of employee conduct.

I hope I shall possess firmness and virtue enough to maintain what I consider the most enviable of all titles, the character of an honest man.

—George Washington

Practicing good business ethics also means being careful not to discuss confidential credit union business outside work. This includes more than just the status of members' accounts and their transactions. It also includes cash drawer amounts, office opening and closing procedures, types of alarms, and other security practices. You may trust the people you talk to but you can't control whom they might tell.

Professional Image

Members form an opinion about the credit union based on your image and appearance. Because a credit union is a financial institution, "businesslike" is the best description of how tellers should dress and look. That is, after all, how members want their accounts handled. Be sure you are aware of and follow your credit union's rules for dress and appearance. Here are a few tips on work attire.

Clothing: Credit unions often adopt employee dress policies that reflect those of the employer groups they serve. If a major sponsor is a conservative insurance company, for example, the credit union would likely require its employees to dress in more formal business attire. On the other hand, if most members are blue-collar workers, they might feel more comfortable among credit union employees in casual attire. Some dress codes today permit employees to wear polo shirts featuring the credit union logo and khaki pants.

If your dress code specifies business attire or business casual, aim for classic styles rather than trendy fashions. Select more muted color combinations and tailored styles. When women wear dresses or skirts, hose are generally expected.

Overall, the look you should be trying to achieve is professional. It may not be "the real you" in your personal life, but at the counter, it commands respect and builds trust. One way to check which styles are most appropriate at your credit union is to observe

---

the clothing that supervisors and managers wear. Ask questions of your supervisor if you're not sure whether a certain outfit would be acceptable. Also, check to make sure your work attire is in good condition and repair.

Grooming: Your clothing is not the only factor that determines the impression you make. Pay attention to your hair and face as members notice these first. Keep your hair clean and appropriately styled. Men who wear a beard or mustache should keep it trimmed. Women should apply makeup conservatively and remember that under your credit union's fluorescent lights, heavy makeup appears more noticeable.

Also, pay attention to your hands. They will be on display constantly as you count back cash, pick up share drafts, and give receipts. Make sure your nails are manicured and clean.

One other factor that influences your appearance is not eating at the teller counter. Even a mint or gum will be noticeable to a member and interferes with a professional manner. Chewing gum makes it hard to talk.

Promptness

A quality that is especially critical in the member service environment is promptness. An adequate number of staff members must be available in the lobby at all times to meet an unpredictable flow of members. Strive to be at work on time every day. Allow yourself enough time to do anything you need to do, so that you are at your window no later than your scheduled time to begin. Likewise, make sure you return from lunch and breaks promptly. In many credit unions, only one teller at a time goes to lunch or a break. Returning late changes the schedule for all other lunches or breaks that day and makes it difficult for supervisors or staff members to make plans or attend meetings. Your promptness helps keep the office running smoothly and is appreciated by everyone.

Promptness goes beyond simple timeliness about starting times. It entails quickly fulfilling your responsibilities such as immediately greeting members at your window. It means meeting deadlines for responding to memos or turning in employment forms such as timesheets, changes of address, or emergency phone numbers, when needed. Promptness in these situations shows you are willing to do your share of the work and are in control of your responsibilities.

Dedication

It is not enough that we do our best; sometimes we have to do what is required.

—Winston Churchill

You show your dedication to the job in many ways. First, an excellent attendance record shows your commitment to the job. This is another way that the member service environment is special in your job. When you are scheduled to work, you are needed. If you're not there, member service may suffer. A replacement has to be found, which means another employee might be pulled from a different area, leaving that department shorthanded. Or, if no replacement is possible, the counter must operate short-staffed. That can overwork your fellow employees and cause members to wait longer.

Although attendance is critical, sometimes unforeseen circumstances occur. Occasionally you miss work due to an illness or other medical need. When you must miss work due to illness, call your supervisor as early as possible to allow time for other arrangements to be made. If possible, try to schedule routine doctor and dentist appointments on days you don't work. Or, before making plans, talk to your supervisor about which day or time would be least inconvenient. For example, another employee might be scheduled for a vacation day and avoiding that day would be better. Check your employee handbook or your credit union's personnel policies for specifics on how these situations are handled in your credit union.

Dedication also means caring about your job and credit union. When the lobby is empty and other tasks have been completed, a dedicated teller will find or ask for other work to do. Dedicated tellers continually look for ways to improve their work. When after-hours help is requested, they volunteer. Dedicated employees may attend credit union functions on their own time. Examples are league or chapter meetings, member education sessions, and annual meetings.

DEVELOPING YOUR SKILLS

In addition to recognizing and improving your teller qualities, you can also develop and extend your job skills. *Skills* are the techniques you use to perform the actions of

---

your job. You develop your skills through training and experience. You are an active player in this process; it's not something that just happens to you. You can get the most out of training and day-to-day job experiences by using the following techniques.

Learn the Teller Job Thoroughly

Whether you are a new or experienced teller, you know there's a lot to the job. Many people new to this job have been heard to exclaim, "I never realized how much tellers do!" Your first priority for achieving job success is learning your job thoroughly. Two techniques are most useful for this: asking questions and taking notes.

Ask Questions

When another employee or job trainer is teaching you part of the job, make yourself an active learner. *Always* ask questions if you don't understand something. Even if you're not sure how to exactly phrase the question, first stop the trainer and at least say you don't understand. Then, try to phrase a question or even just ask if he or she can explain it a little differently. This can be challenging for the trainer but persist until you understand. In the long run, it will be better than if you let the training continue without making sure you understand.

If you think you do understand, don't simply say, "Uh, huh," and nod your head. How can you be sure you always understand? Maybe you misunderstood and don't even know it. At critical points in the training, think of questions to test your under-standing. One way to do this is to stop the trainer and propose an imaginary situation with your explanation of what you think you should do. Then, ask if that's correct. For example, perhaps an employee has just explained how to post a certificate penalty. You think you understand but to verify you could ask, "So, if a member has $5,000 in a two-year certificate and she wants to withdraw $1,000, I would . . ." and then repeat the steps and point to the keys on the terminal that you would press. If you get any-thing wrong, the trainer can give you the correct information. These types of imaginary situations will also help you memorize the correct procedures because they are a form of practice.

Take Notes

When you are learning something new, take notes because it gives you a reference for the future. Also, the act of writing it down helps you learn and remember. When you take notes, make sure you write down the critical points such as function keys or code numbers and verify that they are correct. Sometimes others may get a little impatient when you take notes. Just reassure them that it will save them time in the future because you won't have to ask again. Most people recognize this is true and to their advantage as well.

A final point about taking notes is to make sure you write legibly and adequately. Don't try to hurry to avoid having the other person become impatient. If you scribble a few unintelligible words, it may be worse than taking no notes at all. If you have to write quickly, take the time to rewrite your notes later. Then, you will have a reference that is easy to read in the future.

Develop Judgment

In the process of learning your job, you will learn how to make more complex decisions. You'll develop judgment about what actions to take when the choice is not obvious, especially for member requests. This is when your job becomes challenging but also particularly rewarding.

In general, always consider whether a rule has been established for the situation. Many times, rules are based on federal and state laws, and disregarding them can jeopardize your credit union by causing it to be out of compliance. Fines and other penalties can result. Rules are also established for the safety of funds. Skirting the rules puts funds at risk and negates the trust members have placed in the credit union. Finally, following rules ensures consistency. Because of the credit union's unique democratic philosophy, members expect equal treatment. To apply rules to one member and not another is unfair.

Keep in mind, however, that many policies and procedures are established to give the credit union flexibility in handling accounts. In many ways, they are unique to each individual credit union, based on laws and the best interests of its members.

Here are some tips to help you make sound decisions in these situations:

1. Get the facts. Make sure you understand exactly what the situation is or what the member is requesting.
2. Refer to credit union policies and procedures. Look for direction from established guidelines.
3. Check your notes. It's a good idea to keep important notes in easy reach. A situation may have been discussed at a staff meeting or during training. If so, you may have a record of it. Or, you may have a memo that establishes guidance.

4. Remember past experiences. Think about any previous situations that may have been similar.

5. Look for consistency. Ask yourself if what you plan to do is consistent with other credit union practices. Will the request be unfair to other members? Will it cause a problem in the future because it establishes a precedent? Is there a cost to the credit union?

6. Ask for advice. If you have any doubt, *check with your supervisor.* If you have even the smallest question, you will make a better decision if you seek guidance. You'll also learn whether your supervisor feels you should make this type of decision again in the future.

Be Open to Change

When one door closes, another opens; but we often look so long and so regretfully upon the closed door that we do not see the one which has opened for us.

—*Alexander Graham Bell*

Throughout your employment, changes will keep occurring in services, procedures, fees, policies, and just about any other area you can think of. When changes occur, keep an open mind and look for the positive consequences. For most people, the negative aspects (if there are any) will quickly come to mind. However, to deal most effectively with change, make sure you don't discount the positive effects and concentrate only on the negatives. Most changes have both and you should seek a balance.

For example, your credit union might change its hours. Perhaps it will be open longer on certain days while reducing the hours on other days. The change in your work schedule could be an inconvenience and might mean you have to make changes in a family schedule. On the other hand, the longer hours might mean that you're less overworked and frazzled on those days because the member traffic is spread out more.

Look for Self-Development Opportunities

Find ways to increase your value as a teller through self-improvement. Additional training, attendance at credit union functions, and assumption of more duties are all ways to improve yourself. By completing additional training, you demonstrate a desire to excel in what you do. Many credit unions today cross-train employees to handle jobs in different departments and/or branches. CUNA & Affiliates and your state league provide many training opportunities. In addition, you can create your own educational opportunities by participating in other training programs offered at your credit union or attending classes at a local college, university, or technical school. Training prepares you for greater responsibilities, and handling more responsibilities displays both skill and dedication.

In short, continue to reinforce your reputation as a valuable employee. Careful handling of accounts and a desire for self-improvement will add much to your value as a teller.

LOOK TO YOUR FUTURE

This handbook has introduced you to the concepts and skills you will need to succeed as a teller. By no means, however, does it contain everything you need to learn. No book does. Much of what you need to develop into an excellent teller comes from the experiences you will encounter every day as you serve members. Additional support comes from coworkers, sharing with you their experiences and understanding. The purpose of this handbook is to guide you through the maze of basic knowledge and emphasize the areas of greatest importance.

Ultimately, the success you achieve in your job depends on you. You're the one whose skills and energy are put to work every day serving members. You're the one who must decide, after absorbing all the information this handbook offers, what you will use from it. And you're the one who will demonstrate your commitment to the credit union's philosophy of mutual self-help, democratic decision making, and not-for-profit service.

Remember, when it comes to service professions, being a teller is one of the most important positions you can hold. Many people depend on you to provide efficient, accurate, and courteous service under conditions that can sometimes create stress. You have the opportunity to make a positive impact on each of these people whether you do so with a simple smile, a friendly remark, a suggestion on how to save money, or a cautious decision that protects funds. As a result, you'll find your job to be challenging, rewarding, and enjoyable.

Finally, keep in mind that your job as a teller is constantly changing and has many opportunities. Each day will present new opportunities for you to learn and grow, both informally on the job and through formal education and training. You also may have the chance for promotion. Although you possess strong qualifications for promotion to a member service representative, you must also demonstrate how your continued employment will help the credit union.

The key is being open to opportunities. If you are, you'll find yourself looking forward to what each day as a credit union teller will bring.

CHECK IT OUT! ✔

Your Teller Qualities

Directions: Review the teller qualities in this chapter and also consider other important qualities you bring to the job. List three qualities that you think you have particular talent for. Then, list three qualities on which you'd like to improve. Discuss your talents and goals with your supervisor.

Three Teller Qualities I Have

1.

2.

3.

Three Teller Qualities I Want to Improve

1.

2.

3.

Your Future

Directions: Find out about further training and education opportunities available through your credit union or other local source. Consider which opportunities will improve your skills as a teller. Make plans to take advantage of these opportunities and discuss them with your supervisor.

THE CREDIT UNION SYSTEM

YOU'RE PART OF AN INTERNATIONAL NETWORK

The credit union system is a network of membership and service organizations that exists solely to support the services and benefits provided to members.

People in the credit union movement have taken the idea of mutual self-help and applied it to solving many of the unique challenges credit unions face. All around the world, we organize ourselves into groups to accomplish on behalf of many what our individual organizations probably couldn't do on their own.

Most credit unions choose to join this *credit union system*. The system is a network of membership and service organizations that helps train and educate staff and volunteers, offers advice and counsel, provides financial services at economies of scale, and works for credit unions' interests in state and federal legislatures.

The affiliated organizations in the credit union system extend from local groups to an international confederation. Through the system, members in your credit union are connected with people all over the globe who are trying to make their lives a little better. Figure A.1 shows how the credit union system fits together.

THE CORE OF THE SYSTEM

Members are the most important group in the credit union system. They are the focal point for various organizations that exist to provide members with a wide range of services and benefits.

Figure A.1 Credit Union System

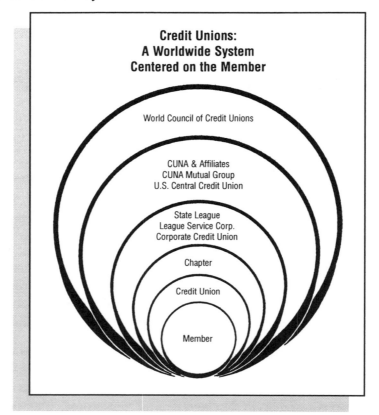

Individual members band together to create an organization they control, known as a **credit union.** This organization provides a safe place for them to save, a source of credit attuned to their needs, and other services that help them make the most of their financial resources.

LOCAL/STATE ASSOCIATIONS

A **chapter** is a local organization of credit unions. Chapters meet monthly for educational and professional development purposes; they also gather to recognize chapter members' achievements. Chapters serve specific geographic sections of a state, and they're often the most accessible source of face-to-face networking opportunities for credit union employees and volunteers.

State leagues are nonprofit trade associations organized to (1) help you and your credit union with problems, (2) meet your educational and informational needs, (3) work for your legislative interests at the state level, and (4) provide a link for your credit union with the rest of the system.

As not-for-profit organizations, leagues have certain limits on the types of services they can offer. To meet more of credit unions' specialized needs, many leagues have formed for-profit service corporations, known as **league service corporations.** These subsidiaries act as advertising agencies, data processing services, market researchers, investment advisers, insurance services, and more.

A **corporate credit union** is a credit union *for* credit unions. Most of the thirty-plus corporate credit unions operate within single states, though some now serve several states. Each gives its member organizations the ability to take advantage of economies of scale and diversification in managing their funds, rather than investing in or borrowing from for-profit institutions. Corporate credit unions also provide access to efficient financial and payment services.

SERVICES AT THE NATIONAL LEVEL

Membership in the state league makes your credit union part of a national organization, known as **CUNA & Affiliates.** Credit Union National Association (CUNA) is a nonprofit trade association that provides programs and services on a national basis for leagues and credit unions. These include educational and training materials, workshops and schools, magazines and newsletters, research, public relations, legislative support, and new product development.

Other organizations affiliated with CUNA help expand the scope of services provided at the national level. These include various transaction and support services, as well as custom printing of forms, specialty items, programs for the young and old, and more.

CUNA Mutual Group offers different types of insurance and financial services products to credit unions and their members throughout the world.

U.S. Central Credit Union is a credit union for the corporate credit unions. U.S. Central offers investments, lending, and payment services for the corporates, just as the corporates provide them for individual credit unions.

YOUR LINK TO THE INTERNATIONAL CREDIT UNION COMMUNITY

The **World Council of Credit Unions** is the international organization of credit unions and financial cooperatives. It supports the growth of credit unions and cooperative ideals in nearly ninety countries through various technical, development, and member services.

GLOSSARY

Accounting department Employees who classify and post all transactions to the credit union's general ledger.

Charter A credit union's license to operate, granted by either the state or federal government.

Collateral Something of value pledged to secure a loan; the vehicle is generally identified as collateral for an auto loan, while a house is collateral for its mortgage.

Collections department Employees who contact members who are behind on loan payments to make arrangements to repay their obligations.

Cooperative A not-for-profit organization owned and controlled by members; a credit union is a financial cooperative.

Credit card A plastic card that represents a line of credit, or approved maximum amount a member can borrow over a future period.

Credit committee Loan officers (and, in some credit unions, volunteers) who decide whether to approve loan applications.

Debit card Convenience service that resembles a credit card but works like an electronic share draft.

Direct deposit Authorization by a member to an employer to deposit paycheck directly in member's credit union account.

Embezzlement Theft of credit union funds by an employee.

Field of membership The groups whose members may join a credit union, such as employees of specified companies or residents in a certain geographic area.

Float The value of account balances created by the time it takes to clear checks.

Forgery Fraudulent alteration of a share draft or check on which the drawer's signature is not genuine.

Hold Temporary restriction on a payment of all or any part of the balance in an account.

Home equity loan Type of loan using the value of a home above and beyond the mortgage amount as collateral for borrowing.

Individual retirement accounts (IRAs) Special accounts established by Congress to provide tax-deferred savings.

Information services department Employees who install and maintain computer hardware, software, and online services.

Investment department Employees who offer share certificates, individual retirement accounts, money market accounts, and other special savings products.

Kiting Attempting to draw against uncollected or nonexistent funds for fraudulent purposes.

Loan department Employees who take and process credit applications, submit them for decisions, inform members of those decisions, complete loan documents, and close the loans.

Members The people who own and control a credit union; they are both owners and customers.

Money market accounts High-yield accounts that usually require a high minimum balance but provide greater flexibility in fund access than do share certificates.

Mortgage A loan secured by real estate.

National Credit Union Administration The agency that supervises and regulates all federally chartered credit unions.

Payroll deduction Authorization by a member to transfer a portion of paychecks directly to a share or loan account.

Payroll deduction department Employees who track and apply the amounts members designate to be deposited automatically into their accounts from their paychecks; may be part of the accounting department.

Policies Guidelines approved by the board of directors that direct credit union operations.

Post-dated Refers to checks dated later than the current day; they should not be honored.

Procedures Step-by-step methods for handling important credit union operations.

Refinancing Taking out a new loan to repay an existing loan with a higher interest rate.

Share accounts Regular saving accounts people must open to become credit union members.

Share certificates Savings accounts that must be maintained for a set period to avoid penalty; typically these accounts pay higher dividends and require a higher minimum balance than share or share draft accounts.

Share draft accounts Accounts from which members may withdraw funds by completing forms called "share drafts"; similar to checking accounts offered by banks.

Share draft department Employees who track members' share draft accounts by preparing and sending drafts through the clearing system, ordering new share drafts, placing stop payments, handling overdrafts, and producing monthly statements.

Special purpose accounts Savings products that allow members to save for specific purposes, such as paying for holiday spending, education, or taxes.

Stale-dated Refers to checks that, because they are dated before a previous date established by the credit union (typically three or six months earlier), cannot be honored.

I N D E X

information services departments, 11–12
insurance, on loans, 27
internal controls, 82–83
Internet services, 28–29
interruptions, 70, 75
investment departments, 11
irate members, 46–49

J

jargon, 39, *40–41*
judgment
    developing, 107–8
    reserving, 61

K

kidnappings, 97–98
kiting, 86–87

L

language difficulties, 55
league service corporations, 115
lines, *47*, 49–50
listening
    active, 44, 106
    to irate members, 48
loan companies, versus credit unions, *5*
loan departments, 11
loans, types of, *23*, 25–27

M

management, relating to, 13–15, 62–65, 66
marketing departments, 12–13
maturity dates, *41*
member relations process, 42–46
members
    angry, 46–49
    as credit union owners, 2–3, 113–14
    disabled and elderly, *47*, 52–53
    education programs for, 29–30
    sudden illnesses of, 93–94
    tellers' responsibilities to, 6–8, *9*, 14
        (*see also* member service)

member service
    correcting mistakes, 76–78
    guidelines for, 36–41
    procedures for, 42–46
    special situations, 46–53
    tellers' role in, 6–8, *9*, 14
microprinting, 85
mistakes. *See* errors
money market accounts, 25
mortgages, 26–27

N

names, using, 43–44
National Credit Union Share Insurance
    Fund (NCUSIF), 6
natural disasters, 96
negotiable instruments, *41*
new members, *47*, 54
nonverbal communication, 42–43
note-taking, 106–7
not-for-profit orientation, 3

O

older members, *47*, 53
online services, 28–29
organization charts, *4*
overdraft protection, 27

P

paraphrasing, 44
payroll deduction, 28
payroll deduction departments, 10–11
people orientation, 101–2
personal identification numbers (PINs), *41*
personal loans, 26
personal transactions, 82–83
points, *41*
policies
    explaining to members, *47*, 51
    against fraud, *88*
    and individual judgment, 107–8
    supporting, 13–14
    See also procedures

tellers
desirable traits of, 101–5
responsibilities to members, 6–8
work with management, 13–15, 62–65, 66
work with other departments, 8–13
terms, *41*
tiered rates, *41*
training opportunities, 108–9, 110
transactions
explaining, 54
procedures for, 42–46
transit numbers, *41*

U

U.S. Central Credit Union, 115

V

verification, 70, 72
volunteers, 4

W

watermarks, 85
web sites, 30
World Council of Credit Unions, 116

Credit Union Board of Directors Handbook, #22824-JK1
Third Edition

Helps your directors build confidence and gain shared understandings which lead to a united, purposeful board. Provides information on: board of directors profile—legal liabilities; conflict of interest; insurance protection; becoming an effective director; duties and responsibilities; board's role in relation to other committees and staff; how to establish and maintain a good relationship with your credit union's chief executive officer; how to improve communications with members, management, and committees.

$24.95   1999

Credit Union Call Center Handbook, #22259-JK1

Guides you through the development, implementation, and evaluation of a credit union call center, and explores critical issues in development, operations, and management. Covers call center background, objectives, transactions and marketing, technology applications and integration, cost-benefit considerations, call processing and procedures development, staffing, burnout prevention, and coaching. Appendices provide call center statistics, procedure and observation forms, performance standards, and a business plan.

117 pages $29.95   1999

The CUSO Handbook, #22267-JK1

Credit Union Service Organizations offer a unique opportunity to do more for members. CUSOs have proven their value by enabling credit unions to enhance member services, rein in operational costs and develop new partnerships. This book explores the variety and versatility offered by the CUSO structure, along with legal and operational issues. Also covers using a CUSO to do more for members, effectively organizing a CUSO, meeting legal and regulatory requirements, member services and operational CUSO opportunities, applying business planning principles, and learning from the experiences of successful CUSOs.

151 pages $29.95   1999

Director's Handbook for Credit Union Examinations, #21782-JK1

This handbook helps directors understand the NCUA examination process, examiner concerns, and examination preparation. Chapters include overview of the exam process, director and management preparation, on-site examination scope, CAMEL rating system, and the joint conference and examination report. Also included are relevant NCUA documents, checklists, and examples of problems as well as strategies to remedy these problems.

128 pages $29.95   1999

Director's Handbook for Credit Union Regulations, #21310-JK1

The more directors know about the laws and regulations that govern credit unions, the better they can perform their jobs. This handbook gives directors the regulatory information they need in a style that is easy to read and fast paced. Chapters cover the laws and regulations affecting credit unions, rules for the organizational structure of federal credit unions, regulatory requirements associated with maintaining federal share insurance, consumer protection regulations and laws governing credit union operations, general lending regulations, including NCUA and Federal Reserve Board regulations, and information on additional resources.

128 pages $29.95   1999

Credit Union Marketing Handbook, #21253-JK1

Effective marketing powers successful organizations. Because of the special relationship credit unions have with members, marketing to both current and potential members is especially critical. You'll learn how to: develop marketing strategies for new and existing products, use distribution systems—both direct and indirect—effectively, use advertising, public relations, and sales promotion, develop pricing strategies to ensure growth while fulfilling your mission, formulate marketing objectives and goals, project sales, calculate the return on a marketing investment to track results, develop and manage the marketing process, and write a marketing plan. The appendix includes a marketing plan format.

166 pages $29.95   1998

Credit Union Political Action Handbook, #21305-JK1

Helps guide your credit union in effective political action at local, state, and national levels. Everyone who has the responsibility for safeguarding the future of our credit unions should read this handbook. This includes directors, volunteers, managers, marketers, and staff who handle communications, legislative, or political activities. Beginning with an introduction to the political process, the handbook rapidly moves to describe credit unions in relation to politics, elections, and legislation. It provides case studies in the areas of political process and lobbying. It will help your credit union create and maintain a consistent political presence, rather than rallying efforts only in time of crisis.

109 pages $29.95   1998

Security and Fraud Prevention Handbook for Tellers, #21252-JK1

Explores security concerns relevant to tellers. Useful for other frontline staff like member representatives. Can serve as a template to assist in training and writing policies. Beginning with an overview of security issues, it covers cash handling, counterfeiting, money laundering, check fraud, scams affecting members, internal security, and robbery and other emergencies. Chapters contain real-life examples and self-test activities. A great companion to the *Credit Union Teller Handbook #765.*

144 pages $29.95   1998

Credit Union Supervisory Committee Handbook, #763-JK1
Second Edition

Helps committee members succeed by giving them information on supervisory committee profile qualifications; makeup of the committee; removal from the committee; legal considerations; insurance protection; conflict of interest; duties and responsibilities; supervisory committee relationships—with members, directors, other committee members, management and staff, external and internal auditors, and your regulatory agency.

130 pages $14.95   1997

Credit Union Teller Handbook, #22823-JK1
Third Edition

Helps tellers and member service representatives get started and succeed, and also provides an excellent foundation for advanced training. Includes orientation to credit union uniqueness, teller's role and descriptions of duties and responsibilities, management expectations, policies and procedures, suggestions for handling emergency situations. Self assessments and checklists reinforce key concepts and identify growth opportunities.

93 pages $24.95   1999

Volunteers and Lending, #21222-JK1

Offers a contemporary view of lending trends, committee roles, and the issues facing credit union lenders. Looks at the market forces that are causing credit committees to change, be replaced, or be eliminated entirely. Even though committees are changing, directors and volunteers still have responsibility for sound lending policies and practices. These important duties are outlined, with information and guidelines provided for various positions.

112 pages $29.95   1998

Managing Staff Recruitment: How to Hire the Best and the Brightest, #22258-JK1

Covers relevant employment laws, policies and procedures, job advertisements, preliminary screening, interviewing, and final selection. Also covers

- understanding today's employment environment;
- attracting skilled people;
- recruiting techniques;
- identifying qualified candidates;
- interviewing effectively;
- providing employee orientation.

Your employees are your most valuable resource. *Managing Staff Recruitment* helps you retain a dedicated, long-term work force. Includes sample job application, interview guide, self-evaluation, job descriptions, and more!

181 pages $34.95   1999

Catch Members with the Net: A Guide to Maximizing Web Site Effectiveness, #22261-JK1

This handbook discusses the history, rationale, and uses of a web site, and the key concerns of maintaining and analyzing web site effectiveness. Includes

- basic web site design;
- security and legal issues;
- keeping your content and design fresh;
- tracking your web site's effectiveness;
- marketing your site.

Also included are sample web sites, basic HTML instruction, a sample worksheet, and checklists. Web sites are becoming an integral part of credit union operations and marketing efforts. Learn how to create an effective site for your credit union!

150 pages $34.95   1999

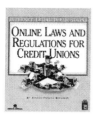

Technocasting for Credit Unions: Identifying Tomorrow's Technology Needs Today, #22260-JK1

Discover the most compelling technology options available in the financial industry today, and learn how to take a systematic approach for your credit union technology decisions. Topics include

- forecasting and planning for technology;
- new and upcoming technologies;
- possibilities and pitfalls of the World Wide Web;
- budgeting for and analyzing performance of technology;
- technology staffing and implementation;
- technology vendors.

Use *Technocasting for Credit Unions* as your credit union resource for making technology decisions. Feel confident that you're using technology to help members take control of their financial lives.

131 pages $34.95   1999

Online Laws and Regulations for Credit Unions: Internet Legal Implications, #22561-JK1

Explores the laws and regulations credit unions must follow in catching the growing wave of Internet commerce. Includes specific examples of how those regulations apply and the consequences of noncompliance. *Online Laws and Regulations* also covers

- general legal principles;
- compliance issues;
- new accounts;
- lending over the Internet;
- electronic funds transfers;
- privacy and security concerns.

Includes a glossary of Internet terms and a reprint of an NCUA *Regulatory Alert* containing the NCUA's opinion on many of the compliance issues that arise in Internet transactions.

120 pages $34.95   1999

Credit Union Branding: Winning Strategies for Marketers, #22640-JK1

Provides the tools you need to meet the challenges of brand marketing. By giving brands distinctive qualities, brand marketers create loyalty for their products and services, and their credit unions. Provides a comprehensive background on the history, strategy, and opportunities of brand marketing. Includes

- the lexicon of branding;
- functional and emotional benefits of brands;
- tactics for implementing a brand marketing program;
- trademark protection;
- brand consistency and revitalization;
- examples of great branding techniques.

Also included is information on the National Credit Union Brand Campaign. Learn how you can effectively manage your credit union brand!

122 pages $34.95   1999

People, Not Profit: The Story of the Credit Union Movement, #22228
Third Edition

First published in 1993, *People, Not Profit* has been one of the most popular versions of the credit union story. This new edition highlights every significant point in American credit union development—from the early years of struggle, through the remarkable growth and development of the last five decades, including how credit unions mobilized to pass H.R. 1151 and preserve the credit union alternative for consumers. It chronicles the persistent challenges from the banking industry—each of them ultimately resulting in grassroots victories for credit unions. This compact manual helps staff understand how each person is an important part of today's credit union movement, prepares people at all levels for the challenges we now face, and its helps convey to members the qualities that can be found only in credit unions.

96 pages $24.95   1999

To place an order or
ask a question:

Call **1-800-356-8010, press 3**
(or dial ext. 4157)
7:30 a.m. to 6:00 p.m.
Monday–Friday, CST

Local calls 608-231-4157

TTY phone 1-800-356-8030

Fax 1-608-231-1869

Mail the order form to:
CUNA Customer Service
P.O. Box 333
Madison, WI 53701–0333

E-Mail customerservice@cuna.com

CUNA & Affiliates Order Form

Ship to:

Credit union

Attention

Street address for shipping

City/State/Zip

Bill to:

Credit union

Attention   Title

Address

City/State/Zip

Phone   Ext. #

Fax

Payment method

☐ Credit unions in U.S.:
No need to prepay, we'll bill you for the total amount of your order.

☐ Individuals and International customers:
Must prepay in U.S. dollars.

Quantity	Stock Number	Description	Unit Price	Total

Subtotal: We'll calculate the freight and handling (plus sales tax if applicable).

Prices subject to change based on reprints and revisions.

Thank you for your order!